S0-BDT-444

Top 10 Reasons You Should Buy This Book

10. You're a Berlioz fan and his caricature is on the cover.

9. I *guarantee* you will be able to find your name in this book.[1]

8. Read the definitive list of Collective Nouns for Musicians.

7. Cheap laughs![2]

6. Discover if you might be a pit musician.[3]

5. You need a new bathroom reader.[4]

4. This book includes a free picture of Miss June, 2014.

3. You will learn the answers to two of our generation's most controversial mysteries.[5]

2. Bring this book to any of my performances and I'll give you a free backstage tour, then at intermission you can come to the rail of the pit and be one of the cool people who knows one of the musicians.

1. It makes a great gift for aspiring musicians—hurry, before it's too late to save them from a life in the pits.

---

[1] Guaranteed or your money back.

[2] *War and Peace, The Great Gatsby,* and *Moby Dick,* for example, all cost far more money in terms of laughs per page.

[3] Page 47.

[4] Laxative effect *not* guaranteed.

[5] Pages 86 and 111.

Life in the Pits

or

"It's OK, I'm with the Band"

by

Frank Meredith

SAVANNAH BOOKS

Copyright ©2014 Frank Meredith
All rights reserved.

No part of this book may be reproduced, stored in a retrieval system, or transmitted by any means, electronic, mechanical, photocopying, recording, or otherwise, without written permission from the publisher.

Design and composition by Frank Meredith

Cover illustration: "Un concert à mitraille et Berlioz" by Jean Ignace Isidore Gérard (1803-47). First published in *L'Illustration*, on November 15, 1845. Public domain image. Colorized by Frank Meredith.

Rear cover photo by Alyse French: www.AlyseFrenchPhotographyBlog.com

ISBN-13: 978-0984396115
ISBN-10: 098439611X

Printed in the United States of America on acid-free paper

First edition published 2014
Savannah Books, New York
savannahbooksinc@gmail.com

FIRST EDITION

For my fellow pit denizens past, present, and future;

But especially for Maestro Charles Schneider,

Founding Music Director at Glimmerglass Opera

And one of upstate New York's greatest musical treasures.

Table of Contents

My first gig (see page 45.)

Prelude

Not everyone can play quarterback. Or pitch. Or play point guard. For every Tom Hanks or Meryl Streep, a movie will have dozens, hundreds, or even thousands of "little guys," without whom the stars would shine less brightly. So it goes in the musician's world. Sure, I'd pay big money to hear Itzahk Perlman or Katherine McPhee or Brian Stokes Mitchell perform a concert of unaccompanied music, but I'd pay even more to hear their glorious sounds enhanced by the colors and dramatic impact of a backup band. I'll even include backup vocalists with that.

Remember in the movie *Amadeus*, when Mozart's rivals rat him out on his use of ballet in a new opera, resulting in the scene where Mozart has the dancers rehearse the ballet without music? Ridiculous! Even Nureyev and Baryshnikov would have looked like prancing twits without music, and the Sugar Plum Fairy would look like she's tiptoeing through a minefield.

I'll concede that piano, organ, and guitar soloists can provide their own "backup band," but add some brass and percussion to Diane Bish on a cathedral organ and not only could you bring down the house, you could take down the walls of Jericho. Admit it, Diana Ross was better with *The Supremes*, just like Michael Jackson was nothing without *The Jackson...* well, never mind on that one, but he did have a heck of a backup band throughout his career.

Playing second fiddle to a headliner is no easy task; ask Doctor Watson or Robin, the Boy Wonder. But when that second fiddle is a finely tuned and superbly coordinated partner, then the star can really shine. And oh, the stories that second fiddle could tell! Or the second trombone, in the case of Nanki-Poo in *The Mikado*. Or even the third trombone—the bass trombone, in my case.

Herein you will find many anecdotes and creations from my forty-six years as a sideman in a wide variety of musical styles and venues. Not all of these performances placed me in a "pit," although you will read about times I wish I had been buried in one. I hope you enjoy these glimpses of life back stage—and in that abyss below the stage where small creatures and large insects go to die. Names will be changed to protect the innocent. Or not, we'll have to wait and see...

Disclaimer #1: Why should I be the one to write this book? You might suppose there are any number of musicians whose careers have set them in the shadows of much more prestigious stars and in the nether regions of more famous venues. You suppose correctly. But while they are raking in the dough, collecting royalties, and hobnobbing with world-class musicians and conductors, they miss out on the real joy in life: struggling through your day job while trying to schedule free-lance gigs around your part-time gigs.

Seriously, though, I have plenty of delusions of grandeur, but the multitudinous sales of this book are not among them. My hope is that you will find these anecdotes and creations entertaining, and that my descendants might gain some insight into those odd personality quirks they've inherited and appreciate that love of music is a long-standing family tradition. The Meredith family tree has been rooted in music since the name Merdydd sprouted in Wales centuries ago. It continues to thrive, in spite of those few odd branches that we don't discuss in public. And, of course, I'm hoping my friends and colleagues will be curious enough to buy the book to see which of them appear in the stories.

Disclaimer #2: I promise that every story you are about to read is as accurate as I can portray it. That said, memories change and fade with time. Hopefully, I've been able to omit embellishments and stick with the facts. To anyone who was also a part of these memories: if you remember them differently, drop me an email at LifeInThePitsBook@gmail.com and set me straight.

Disclaimer #3: A lot of these experiences and creations took place in Cooperstown, N.Y. at Glimmerglass Opera, renamed the Glimmerglass Festival in 2011. The opera company is in no way liable for any of what you are about to read.

Disclaimer #4: For the thematic purposes of this book, anyone who plays an accompanying instrument behind a leading performer or group is a "pit musician."[6]

Author's Photo by Nathan Lawrence, October 2012

---

[6] Not to be confused with "mitt position," which is first base or catcher.

The Young Person's Guide to the Pit

Sometimes I like to hang around during the intermission and observe the folks who come down front to peer into the pit. I especially enjoy it when parents bring their children to teach them about the instruments—or is it to warn them about what could happen to them someday if they goof off in school? The misinformation shared often reminds me of my favorite cartoon strip, *Calvin and Hobbes*, when Calvin's father teaches him a mixture of fact and fantasy. So to better equip you on your next trip to the pit, here are some tips you may find helpful.

The best time to visit a pit is about ten minutes before the show begins. By this time, most of the musicians have already emerged from their shelter under the stage and have taken their places around the little platform located front and center in the pit. This platform is called a *podium*[7]; it is where the *maestro*[8] stands. You will see a metal shield on a pole in front of the podium. This is used to protect the maestro from the pointy end of violin bows. Do you see the stick laying on the shield? That is called a *baton.*[9] The maestro uses the baton to control the musicians, lest they wander off. The baton is also used to attract the attention of the performers on stage, though few of them are so easily distracted.

Here is an easy tip on how to determine if the musicians form a "pit orchestra" or a "pit band." If you see a big drum set, electronic instruments, and shiny metal horns, then this is a pit band. If at least half of the musicians have instruments made of wood, then this is a pit orchestra. A good way to remember this is that *orch*ard and *orch*estra are very similar words; and while an orchard has lots of woods that hold fruit, an orchestra has lots of fruits that hold wood.

That cacophony you hear is the musicians warming up their instruments. While the string players loosen up their pitching arms, woodwind players make sure their reeds are moist, percussionists decide which sticks will produce the most noise, harpists pluck their harpstrings to make sure they do not remain in tune, keyboard players let their fingers roam freely up and down the keyboard, and brass players produce more notes than they will play the rest of the night. Eventually, one instrument—an oboe or piano, most likely—will play a single long note. This signals the other players that it is time to settle down and join in on that note, or else the maestro will come in and use the baton on them. This is also the signal for you to hurry back to your seat because the show is about to begin.

---

[7] *Podium* is Latin for "Hey, look at me!"

[8] *Maestro* is Italian for animal trainer.

[9] *Baton* is French for "Don't make me come over there!"

The next best time to visit the pit is during the intermission. While most of the musicians go off in search of such necessities as food, water, and breathable air, a few often remain behind in the pit. They may seem docile, perhaps reading a book or doing a crossword puzzle, but do not presume there is no danger.

Do not reach into the pit.

Do not bounce coins off the timpani.

Do not throw things into the tuba bell. (Exception: wadded up U.S. currency may be used for this purpose.)

Do not feed the brass players. They need to learn how to take care of themselves, and you do *not* want them to follow you home.

Special warning: if you see a double-reed player in the pit during intermission it is because their reed is acting up, and he or she is scraping away at the obstinate *#^+&% in the eternal quest to discover the mythical being known as the "perfect reed." If a knife-wielding double-reed player smiles at you, be advised that this is not a "Hello-thanks-for-stopping-by" smile. Avoid eye contact and slowly back away.

The worst time to visit the pit is after the show has ended. By the time you get there, the brass players will already be in their cars, the percussionists will have covered up their instruments and hidden their sticks, and the string players will be icing their pitching arms backstage. All that will be left in the pit are overturned chairs, music stands knocked awry, and woodwind players swabbing gallons of moisture from the nooks and crannies of their instruments.

If you are really lucky, you may be able to sight one of these rare instruments that may have wandered into the pit.[10]

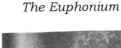

The Euphonium

The author rehearsing "Bydlo" from Pictures at an Exhibition, 1984.

---

[10] See page 128 for links to videos of these instruments in action.

Euphonium is Greek for "good sound." Its basic tubing length is nine feet, the same as the trombone; but since its tubing is conical and it has a larger bell than the trombone, the tone quality is much more mellow. As the baritone voice of the tuba family, it is an important member of bands, brass bands, and brass ensembles. Since the early 1970s it has become an increasingly popular solo instrument, with a great many new and exciting concerti, sonatas, and other solo works being written, performed, and recorded. Prior to the early 1970s, eh...not so much. Orchestrally, Richard Strauss used it in *Don Quixote* and *Ein Heldenleben,* Gustav Holst used it to good effect in *The Planets*, and it is often used to play the "Bydlo" movement in *Pictures at an Exhibition.* I had the pleasure of playing the euphonium in the premier performance and recording of George Lloyd's *Symphony No. 11.* (More on that later.) Only a few operas call for the euphonium. Fortunately, I had the chance to play one at Glimmerglass Opera, Jack Beeson's chilling *Lizzie Borden.*

Note to living composers—even you dead ones, if there's a chance you can find a way to help with this crusade—why not be the envy of your colleagues and include the euphonium in your music? Its gorgeous tone quality and amazing technical dexterity are sure to enhance your compositions in ways beyond your imagining. Believe me, I've imagined it lots of times.

The Contrabassoon

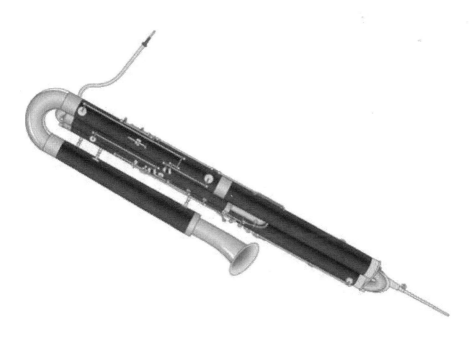

The contrabassoon is exactly double the size of the normal bassoon. Due to its great length it is tightly wrapped, like your colon after you eat too much triple-cheese pizza. There is no instrument in the orchestra that is as low as this one. If you hear this instrument in a movie soundtrack, you can be sure a weird creature is about to appear, right before your eyes. This is also true if you see an open contrabassoon case backstage. Contrabassoon is the Spanish word for "Central American revolutionary."

The Cimbasso

David Saltzman, Glimmerglass Orchestra, 2013

Just look at that thing! (I refer to the instrument.) This is what happens if you use steroid cream on your trombone slide and a valve oil laced with Human Growth Hormone. No wonder "cimbasso" is the Italian word for "drug fiend." Its tubing is the same length as that of a tuba pitched in F or B-flat—or pitched in the dumpster, if the rest of the pit musicians have their way. Its earliest use dates to Bellini's 1831 opera, *Norma*. Verdi used it in several operas because he preferred its sound over that of a tuba. Puccini used it only once— a man who learned from his mistakes. A common misconception is that further use was banned by the Geneva Conventions. Cimbasso parts are sometimes played on a tuba or contrabass trombone. It is always played by the most intrepid member of the brass section.

The Theorbo

Miss June
Theorbo Lovers' *magazine, 2014*

The theorbo was developed in Florence, Italy during the 1580s in order to provide a bass lute sound in the opera orchestra and to accompany solo melodic lines. It is a plucked instrument of the lute family, related to the archlute. Theorbos have a much larger body than a lute, a much longer neck, and a second peg box. One might suspect it is a lute on steroids, but since musicians don't use drugs this is probably not true. Theorbo is French for, "I feel inferior to other lute players, how might I compensate for that?" (French is such a rich language, isn't it?)

My First Pit

My initiation to life in the pits came in the autumn of 1967. During my freshman year in high school,[11] I played trombone for the musical *Little Mary Sunshine*, a spoof on various operettas, which had enjoyed a very successful run of 1,143 performances on Broadway in the early 1960s. Three of the main characters in the show were Chief Brown Bear, the comically misnamed Fleet Foot, and the malevolent Yellow Feather. Their "Indian dialogue" consisted of stereotypical

---

[11] Hanover High School, Hanover, PA.

gibberish, but no one in that day and age seemed to take the least bit of offense.

There is a scene where Fleet Foot, often portrayed as elderly and feeble, goes off stage to feed the horses down by the lake. Always looking for the humor in things, I suggested to the director that I thought it would be funny if a few moments after Fleet Foot exits, there is the sound of a loud splash off stage. The director frowned at the lowly freshman and didn't deign to give a reply. He did not use my suggestion.

Flash forward forty years to the spring of 2007. I had the pleasure of portraying Chief Brown Bear in a community theater production in Clifton Park, N.Y. That show's director loved my off-stage splash idea and used it. The splash elicited a chuckle at all seven performances.

In the intervening years, the gibberish dialogue had been updated to consist of actual Lakota words. There is a scene where the Chief instructs his adopted Indian son, Corporal Jester, about the Lakota language. The director liked my idea of using a flip chart and pointer, so I used crudely drawn animals to teach the actual Lakota words to our Corporal Jester, played by the marvelous actor and director Tim Orcutt. On the third and fourth drawings I switched to pig Latin, which became obvious to the audience as I said "At-cay" and "Og-day." The fifth picture flipped over and showed the drawing of a bee. I waited a beat as the audience figured out what was coming, then said, "Ee-bay." It got a good chuckle every night, and I earned an award from the Theater Association of New York State (TANYS) for the role. The TANYS adjudicator remarked how impressed she was that a pit musician would take a successful turn on stage. (Or was that veiled sarcasm?)

My first trombone.

Aim High...Um, Higher Than That!

My freshman year in high school we had a new band director, Chuck Brodie, a terrific trumpet player fresh out of West Chester State. He had the unenviable task of replacing a legend, Mr. Polaski. As usual, auditions were held for seating in each section of the band. I finished second, one point ahead of Ralph Hoffacker, a junior, and a couple of points behind Tom Hoke, also a junior. They were close friends, the oldest members of the section, and took great offense at my having earned the seat between them in the first trombone section. The next rehearsal after the auditions, I started for my new seat but Tom made it clear that the third chair would be mine. I was more than willing to avoid any confrontation.

Placement in the jazz band trickled down from that audition. Tom played lead trombone, Ralph played second, and I played third. I was happy to hide my inexperience with the tricky rhythms while buried in the section.

All went well until the week of a jazz band competition we were to play that October. Apparently, Tom and Ralph had developed quite a conflict with Mr. Brodie, so they threatened to quit the jazz band. Mr. Brodie accepted their offer. He moved me up to first and recruited two other trombone players for the band. I was a bit apprehensive but also thrilled, especially with the featured trombone solo in "59th St. Bridge Song (Feelin' Groovy)." The written jazz solo included two high D's. I had found a great shallow mouthpiece among my father's collection and had no problem nailing those high D's. I don't recall ever missing one, until...

We deliver a screaming performance of Chuck Brodie's arrangement of "Can't Take My Eyes Off of You/Goin' Out of My Head." We groove our way along "59th Street" up to the trombone solo. I stand. I play. I miss the first high D. Badly. I recover on the next phrase. I decide to redeem myself on the other high D. I do not. Epic fail!

The audience groaned so loudly that when we replayed the adjudicator's tape recording on the way home, they could be heard above the sound of the judge's voice. I didn't switch to the bass trombone that day, but the seed had been planted.

Hu Flung Dung

During a sectional rehearsal for the jazz band, Mr. Brodie tried to clarify the proper articulations for the reed section by writing the passage on the chalk board, then forcefully tapping on each pair of notes as he proclaimed, "Tongued! Slurred! Tongued! Slurred! Slung! Turd!..." He froze and grew red with embarrassment. This was

1968, before Barbra Streisand dropped the first F-bomb in the film *The Owl and the Pussycat*. Teachers didn't use such language, especially in front of their students! In my subsequent years as a band director, I've always had to pause and choose my words carefully before attempting to say any combination of "tongued" and "slurred."

The story of the "Slung! Turd!" spoonerism must have made its way to the faculty room, because that same week one of my high school history teachers put this question on a test:

Who is the Premier of Communist China?
    A) Chung King
    B) Mao-Naise
    C) Mao-Tse Tung
    D) Hu Flung Dung

A surprising number of people chose "A," a popular food brand at the time. And yes, Mao-Tse Tung *was* the Premier of China at the time I was asked that question; thanks for reminding me.

You Call This Music?

Mr. Brodie enjoyed an outstanding career as a band director, leading the marching band to several regional championships and one national championship. I also thank him for introducing me to Aaron Copland's *Symphony No. 3*. That piece later played a large part in developing my interest in an orchestral career. During my freshman year he encouraged me to audition for the York Youth Symphony.

My audition piece was Arthur Pryor's theme and variations on "Blue Bells of Scotland." It is such a standard part of the care and feeding of the aspiring trombonist that it has almost become a cliché. This was my first audition and I was extremely nervous, even though I had performed the piece very well in the District Band tryouts earlier that year. The piece opens with an octave leap from middle C to high C. (And we all remember how much I enjoy excursions into the high range.) Sure enough, I missed the high C on my first try. And the 2nd. And the 3rd. My frustration must have shown because honestly, I *never* had trouble with that before. The lead auditioner waved me off and said, "We're running behind schedule." My heart sank! "I can tell you are a little nervous." Thank you, Captain Obvious. "Anyone who can play this piece is clearly qualified to play third trombone for us." Um, I hadn't exactly played it, had I? Or was that a snarky comment revealing his opinion of third trombones?

Nevertheless, I enjoy a freebie as much as the next guy, so I gratefully accepted the position.

The first rehearsal was a revelation. I don't recall the pieces that were on my stand. All I can say is that I was used to the trombone parts in band, jazz band, and brass ensemble, where I played nearly all of the time. Those composers obviously had a deep appreciation for and love of the trombone. The stuff in front of me had staff after staff of measures with horizontal bars and numbers over them. "Rests?!?" What was *that* all about?

Typical third trombone part.

I quit after the first rehearsal, giving transportation problems as my excuse. But they found someone to give me a ride. Knowing their strict attendance policy, I told them I had schedule conflicts. That worked. I remember feeling sorry for the poor schmucks who have to play third trombone in an orchestra for a living. Um...yeah.

A Mind is a Terrible Thing to—Oh, Look at That!

Outside of the percussion section and tuba, the bass trombone player must count more measures of rest than any other instrument. Early on I considered myself a professional "accountant." I soon learned how to count measures of rest while reading a book or working a crossword puzzle, my two favorite activities to fend off ennui (an oft-used answer in crossword puzzles.) One opera season I read every Agatha Christie mystery in the order she wrote them, which had the bonus of shedding insight into the vast social changes in England from the First World War through the early 1960s. However, my favorite use of downtime is to watch and listen to my colleagues as they play. One of them even inspired a short story, which will appear at the end of the book.

Great music has always sparked my creativity. In 2002 a friend encouraged me to enter a short story competition. I didn't come close to winning anything, but it did start me on a focused path of writing, culminating in a highly acclaimed Civil War novel and a self-published compilation of two teenagers' experiences during the Battle of Gettysburg that has sold more than 2,000 copies to date. (See shameless plugs at the back of this book.)

From the Acknowledgments in the back of my novel, *The Unfinished Work*: "As the bass trombone player with the Glimmerglass Opera, Catskill Symphony, and Utica Symphony, I often have extended passages in the music during which I do not play. Much of this book was written during those lulls. Thank you to Maestro Charles Schneider and my fellow musicians for creating such a stimulating environment in which to work! A special word of thanks to fellow trombonist Dan Martin, whose timely nudges saved me from many late entrances."

Sometimes my mind wandered off into bizarre places, resulting in a variety of comedic efforts, which I'll intersperse along the way.

Proverbs Through the Eyes of a Bass Trombone Player

The first of these "proverbs" was inspired by an opera intermission debate concerning whether the star soprano could break a crystal glass with her voice. I summed up my position with, "If I were Robert Schuller, I wouldn't invite her to sing at the Crystal Cathedral." The rest are a sampling of the thoughts that coalesced as random synapses fired in my brain during long tacets in the opera.

Those who live in glass houses...shouldn't sing high F's.

You can lead a horse to water but...he may prefer a latte.

The best things in life are...covered with chocolate.

Opportunity seldom knocks...on a euphoniumist's door.

If it walks like a duck and quacks like a duck...it could be a moose on his way to a Halloween party.

A fool and his money are...always welcome at my garage sale.

A bird in the hand is worth...letting go before it poops.

Better the devil you know than...the angel who won't
go out with you.

Scratch my back and I'll...follow you anywhere.

Don't count your chickens until they've...crossed the road.

The grass is always greener...by the fire hydrant.

There are only 24 hours in a...good workweek.

When in Rome...drive on the sidewalk. Everyone else does.

The proof is in the pudding...made with Jack Daniels.

Never put off until tomorrow what you can...palm off on
someone else to do today.

No man can serve two...women shopping for shoes.

A woman's place is...wherever she wants. (My Mama didn't
raise no fool.)

Some People Never Learn: The Unteachables

Back in the early 1960s, ABC-TV ran a crime series called *The Untouchables*, based on the Prohibition-era crime-fighting career of Elliot Ness in 1930s Chicago. Picking up on that theme, students at Hanover High School formulated a unique Halloween parade group they dubbed "The Unteachables." One group of guys dressed as gangsters, toted shot guns, and rode in a vintage coupe, complete with a moll riding on each front fender. The second group dressed as G-men, rode in a similar vintage coupe, and carried shotguns and pistols. In between the two groups marched a small band of brass, saxophone, and percussion, who also dressed the part. I played trombone with them for two seasons, 1967-68.

At various points on the parade route, the band moved to the sides of the street and played the theme to *Peter Gunn*, another popular TV series, while the cops drove up and had a shoot-out with the robbers. The shotgun blasts echoed off the buildings; the smoke and smell of gunpowder hung in the air well after we moved on. The group was very popular at Halloween parades in south central Pennsylvania and won many cash prizes.

Part of the fun was marching with the high school band at the front of the parade, then hurriedly changing clothes while driving back to the start of the route to close out the parade with "The Unteachables." The ability to change clothes while driving became a well-honed skill later in my career. More on that later.

The band used a syncopated drum cadence that has stuck with me to this day; I even taught it to the percussion section of the high school band I directed in the 1980s. The cadence had a name— rude at the time but a highly offensive racial slur today.

"The Unteachables"

Photo courtesy of Susan Mitchell

The 1968 Gettysburg Halloween parade was memorable for two things. There was a hamburger stand north of town that served five burgers for a dollar. One of the G-men, Tom Miller, bet us that he could put an entire burger, bun and all, in his mouth and eat it without gagging. He won the bet. Later, while waiting in the assembly area, Tom pulled out the pipe he had brought as part of his costume. Unfortunately, he had forgotten to bring along any tobacco. Worse, he decided to crumple up a handful of dried leaves he found in the gutter, and then proceeded to light up. Soon after, he nervously told us he couldn't see a thing. We were blocked in on a side street with no idea where the nearest medical help might be. Fortunately, his vision returned before the time came for us to move out. I'm still not sure if it was the leaves or the burger that caused this.

News of the final performance of "The Unteachables" made the national wire services. Sadly, it was not for excellence in entertainment. The guys carrying the shotguns made their own "blanks" by emptying the pellets out of each shell. Evidently, one of the guys had been a bit careless, because at a parade in York, PA, stray pellets hit two bystanders and a police officer. No one was seriously injured, but the group was forced to disband.

Soul'd Out—Until Liberation Day

One of my buddies from the Hanover High School jazz band, sax player Jay Wertz, founded the band *Soul'd Out*, consisting of two singers, guitar, bass, drums, organ, and a horn section of trumpet, trombone, and sax. I was delighted to be invited to play trombone. I shared the responsibility of picking out the horn section parts while repeatedly listening to the original recordings; which was no small feat, using a record player in the days before cassette recorders. I eventually developed my own notation of letter names over symbols representing the rhythm. We played for school dances, block parties, and pool parties, covering the songs of Otis Redding, *The Temptations*, Ike & Tina Turner, and other top 40 songs of the 1960s. Once, nearing the end of a three-hour gig, we had played every song we knew. Having noticed that kids sometimes came up and requested songs, I suggested to our lead singer that he pick a couple of songs we had already done and announce that we'd had requests to repeat them. We escaped ridicule—that time.

I'll never forget the autumn of 1969, when Jay found me playing basketball and excitedly told me about this new album he had just bought: *Chicago Transit Authority. Chicago!* Soon after, I also discovered the music of *Blood, Sweat, and Tears*, *The Ides of March*, and *Chase*. This new fusion of jazz and rock was so much more appealing to our horn section, and our lead singer liked imitating David Clayton Thomas. I hoped we might even be able to do away with our matching white bell-bottoms, puffy shirts, and coordinated dance steps. Our format eventually changed as we worked up the new songs. We changed our name to the much edgier *Liberation*, the title of a song on that first *Chicago* album.

We entered a Battle of the Bands in November of 1969. Each group had to perform a 25-minute set, and a large part of the scoring was based on creativity/musicality. We decided to play nonstop for the twenty-five minutes and composed original transitions between each song. Our set included an eclectic mix of music by *The Grass Roots; The Shirelles; Blood, Sweat, & Tears; Joe Jeffrey; Otis Reading;* and, of course, *Chicago*. We got a lot of applause, but not nearly as avid a response as every other band that played, each of which played hard rock exclusively. The judges went off to tally their votes.

We won with 141 points, beating *Last Revolution* (126), *Gross Body* (116), *Phase One* (115), and *Blues Union (105.)* The crowd went crazy—hooting and booing! Yeah, they were a hard rock crowd. See what happens to your mind on drugs? We were clearly the most talented group that day and deserved to win. We even got our picture taken with Miss York County and a local radio DJ. But we never did get rid of those white bell-bottoms, ties, and puffy shirts.

The artists formerly known as **Soul'd Out.**

Colour My World

A recurring topic will be my enthrallment with the music of *Chicago.* January of 1970 saw the release of their second album, featuring "Ballet for a Girl in Buchannon," a multi-movement work by their trombonist James Pankow, my idol. The songs "Make Me Smile" and "Colour My World" were pared from that work and released as best-selling singles. I quickly learned to play both the piano and flute parts from "Colour My World." Today they are the only songs I can play on either instrument.

In the spring of 1970, Jay Wertz and I decided we'd like to perform the song in a high school talent show. He played flute, I played piano, and Sandi Riebling sang the vocal. By that time, I had already figured out how to play the piano part a half-step higher. At the rehearsal, Jay carefully tuned the flute, then I began to play—a half-step higher than the written key. As you may know, the piano plays a two-bar intro and the entire first verse alone, then the vocalist sings the second verse. The flute plays the third verse with the piano.

Sandi doesn't notice that I am playing a half-step higher as she sings. Then Jay enters. Very flat! He stops and asks for another tuning note. No problem, Jay, glad to help fix that! We begin again. I play my intro and verse. Sandi again sings beautifully. Jay begins to play... FLAT! He looks at his instrument and sputters his apologies. I ask him if he wants to tune again, but the strain in my voice trying to stifle the laughter gives me away.

Sandi and I performed the song again at our high school graduation in June of 1971, this time accompanied on flute by my girlfriend, Dianne Dusman. I did not mess around with the key.

Clams Casino

Musicians often use the word "clam" to refer to a noticeable wrong note they have produced. The origin of such usage is unclear but may have originated in the 18th century, when two bells in a bell tower were accidentally rung at the same time, producing a clamor, or "clam." I call it a "clambake" when an unfortunate performer unleashes a series of wrong notes in the same phrase. There are different species of musical clams:

Slimy clam: A finger slips slightly out of position on a string or wind instrument.

Sticky clam: A valve or key sticks.

Airhead clam: Absent-mindedly bowing the wrong string or fingering the wrong key or valve combination.

Cat clam: A reed refuses to vibrate properly, squealing like a poked cat, or a violinist's bow arm spasms.

Butterfinger clam: A percussionist drops a stick or other implement of destruction, possibly hosting a clambake if it rolls the length of the bells or xylophone.

Hercules clam: A percussionist strikes the instrument so forcefully that it flies off its stand. An impromptu clambake may break out.

Spectacled clam: Your glasses do not focus clearly so you misread a note or accidental.

Mute clam: The note fails to speak.

Trespasser clam: You miscount the rests and enter early.

Egocentric clam: You think the cue for another section was meant for you and you enter early.

Neurotic clam: A particularly difficult note that you've practiced repeatedly, then miss because you spent too much time fretting over it as the time came nearer to play it. Often confused with the:

Acrophobic clam: Missing the high note that sits way up above the staff, taunting you like the demon spawn it is.

Rigor mortis clam: Found most frequently after prolonged rests. Stiff lips produce the wrong pitch and the note cracks or fails to speak.

Murphy's clam: Equipment or physical failure for no apparent reason.

Russian clam: Too much vodka in the water bottle.

Irish clam: Too much whiskey in the water bottle.

German clam: Too much beer in the water bottle.

Cross-legged clam: Too much water in the water bottle.

At Glimmerglass many of the musicians take part in a longstanding tradition: for each clam committed, the offender must donate $1.00 toward funding the season-ending Clam Party for all participants. All of us must remain alert to fend off errors caused by mental lapses—especially risky if one eats a big meal before a 3-1/2 hour opera. Dim lighting in a pit and windy conditions at an outdoor venue have also produced many a clam.

Perhaps the most despised clam is that caused by unclear direction from the person with the baton. Keeping a group of professional musicians together is usually not problematic; however, most operas have passages during which the orchestra must provide short, accented notes or chords to punctuate the vocal line on stage. Most frequently these are *not* in a steady tempo, which calls for the utmost clarity in communication between the maestro, the stage, and the pit. Failure to communicate will most assuredly lead to a clambake.

In order to successfully negotiate these passages, the conductor must give a preparatory gesture that indicates two vital things: when and where the accented note must occur. Usually, the conductor begins his preparatory gesture by flicking the baton to show the *ictus*: the point in the air at which the baton will return in tempo and the loud, accented note will be executed. The rest of the gesture is the "upbeat," performed in the new tempo, during which the musicians breathe and prepare to blast away. The note or chord occurs precisely when the baton returns to that location indicated by the *ictus* during the upbeat.

By now, you have no doubt realized how easy it is for that procedure to go awry. Images of a sinewy maestro, whose contortions are sometimes more entertaining than the music that happens in spite of them, easily spring to mind. I am very happy to report that this type of conducting has been exceedingly rare at Glimmerglass. Unfortunately, one conductor became infamous for pausing at the height of the upbeat, then speeding the baton toward the downbeat, which oftentimes was in a different location than indicated by the *ictus* given during the preparation. This produced what I dubbed Popcorn Punctuations, as the ensuing accent took place in several different milliseconds. These Clam Choruses were impossible to predict because they almost never occurred during rehearsals, seemingly the result of the conductor being caught up in the dramatic moment of the performance. Sadly, there was a lot of head-shaking behind our stands after guessing incorrectly where the downbeat was supposed to happen.

Poor lighting and position of the music were major factors in my personal "Clams Casino" calamity. I played in the backup band for Clint Holmes during his tour stop in Schenectady, NY in May of 2011. Clint was a one-hit wonder back in the 1970s with "I've Got a Nickel" and has since become a highly regarded entertainer in Las Vegas. The band was situated on stage, each of us sitting behind one of those classic dance band stands: a wedge-shaped base with a sloping rack for the music. This is perfect for saxophone and guitar players but an absolute nightmare for brass players who have to negotiate a trombone slide over the top of the rack. To make matters worse, the stand lights they provided were of the dim yellow variety, and no matter which way I squinted, the non-adjustable stand managed to keep the music out of the focus range of my progressive lenses. Sharps and naturals looked identical, which made "courtesy accidentals" a virtual minefield. I made sure to mark each of them boldly above the staff, fearing the inevitable clam if I missed even one.

Mr. Holmes put on a truly exceptional show! His medley of tunes from *West Side Story*, accompanied primarily by the drum set, was simply amazing. Sweating bullets, I managed to successfully alternate between staring at my music long enough to memorize the next lick, then glancing up at the conductor to make sure I entered with precision. The show was one of my top ten favorite experiences playing in a backup band. Well, it would have been, but...

We get to the final number on the program. It builds to one of those big, Vegas-style, emotional climaxes. I look down to double-check my note: a low, brassy something-or-other in every bass trombonist's wheelhouse. Clint holds the penultimate note. I glance up at the conductor, waiting for the cue to let 'er rip. He shows the upbeat. I tank up with air. The baton begins its final approach. I hit the last note in perfect timing with Clint.

"Oh, somewhere in this favored land the sun is shining bright;
The band is playing somewhere, and somewhere hearts are light,
And somewhere men are laughing, and somewhere children shout;
But there is no joy in..."
(*Casey at the Bat*, Ernest Thayer)

Somehow, I had forgotten that *only* Clint hits that last note, holds it, and *then* the band plays its big chord as the icing on the cake. Only this time, he has a little help. OK, make that a lot of help. From a friend in low places.

Ithaca College trombone professor, Hal Reynolds, has dubbed such events "premature articulations." There is no medicine for that.

Too bad. Because on the encore I made the same exact mistake! I had been so caught up in his performance that I didn't remember this ending was also different than usual.

I sat dumbfounded through Mr. Holmes' well-deserved curtain calls, then hurried off stage to find him and apologize, explaining that I had been so caught up in the music that I had come in when it felt right, rather than when notated. He smiled, shook my hand warmly, and graciously forgave me. We even became Facebook friends. Mr. Holmes is a classy performer and an even classier human being.

Valve Cello

My string career began with the cello during the 3rd grade. It also ended in the 3rd grade. I remember carrying the cello back and forth to school a few times and sitting with it in front of a music stand, but I don't recall ever producing a sound anyone would have called music. Nevertheless, the cello has been an important part of my musical life, from "borrowing" its solo literature to perform on the euphonium to imitating its bowing techniques in my articulations.

In junior high I dabbled with the baritone horn and wound up playing it in the high school band my senior year. That same year, the high school choir performed *The Messiah*, accompanied by the school orchestra. Lacking enough cello players, the orchestra director asked me to play the part on the baritone horn. The truly odd thing was the music: it often had a few tic-tac-toe marks at the beginning of the staves. I tried not to get distracted by them.

Near the end of a particularly tedious choir rehearsal of the "Hallelujah Chorus," I talked one of my fellow basses into joining me in spicing up the final chord: I sang the 6th, he sang the 9th. Imagine that big, final "Hallelujah." Now make the resolution a jazz chord. Oh, how we laughed. The director, Miss Craft, was not amused.

You Can Tune a Piano, But You Can't Tuna Fish

Playing in tune is of paramount importance to any musician so, of course, it is the subject of many jokes and snarky comments. Here are a couple of my favorites:

During the first season at the Alice Busch Opera Theater at Glimmerglass, a heating system had not yet been installed in the pit. There is a clause in the orchestra's contract which states the musicians cannot be required to play if the temperature drops below a certain level, since the strings in particular would have difficulty playing in tune. Sure enough, one July night the temperature dropped into the 40s. The performance stopped while interns and other personnel searched for space heaters. A few of the string players griped about pitch problems, so I suggested, "It might help if you took off your mittens."

Snarky comment #2: The oboist is tasked with providing a tuning pitch of A, vibrating at precisely 442 times per second. Between the constant back pressure from trying to blow the air through the reed—they usually must exhale before inhaling, what's up with that?—and the inevitable adjustment of their handmade reeds, it is truly a wonder that the news isn't filled with stories of oboists "going postal." Once, while tuning at a community orchestra rehearsal, the oboist's reed emitted an obstinate whine. Over a chorus of snickers someone commented, "What was *that*?" To which I replied in my best Fonzie voice, "AAaayy 442."

True Confessions: My Centerfold Appearance

Picture this: The ice rink at Rockefeller Center in New York, December 22, 1974. The golden statue of Prometheus presides as more than 200 euphoniums and tubas play Christmas carols in four- to six-part harmony. The glorious sound gathers in the icy pit, takes flight, and echoes off the skyscrapers of midtown Manhattan. It's like a scene right out of the Phantom of the Opera's most demented fantasy. Or maybe what Godzilla, King Kong, the Kraken, and Mothra would sound like if they formed a barbershop quartet? It's the second annual "Merry Tuba Christmas," conducted by Paul LaValle, director of the *Band of America*.[12]

I noticed a photographer snapping pictures during the concert. I had already managed to position myself in the second row, directly behind two cute female euphoniumists, but there wasn't

---

[12] Several dozen cities now host a Merry Tuba Christmas every December— which leaves thousands of other cities where you may still do your Christmas shopping in peace.

enough room to properly photobomb the shot. No big deal. I figured, at best, the photos might appear on a back page of one of my favorite quarterlies, *The T.U.B.A. Journal,* circulation c. 1,200.

Historical sidebar: T.U.B.A. stands for Tubists' Universal Brotherhood Association, an international organization founded in 1973 to expand the literature, increase performing opportunities, and improve public awareness of music for the tuba and euphonium. There had been debate as to whether the word should be "Tubists" or "Tubaists." (As humor columnist Dave Barry often says, "I am not making this up.") Evidently, since so many of us relied in part on our plumbing skills for our financial well-being, "Tubists" prevailed. Years later, tired of the never-ending flood of junk mail from plumbing supply houses and calls for emergency repairs, the organization changed its name to International Tuba Euphonium Association, ITEA. Now they get calls for furniture you must assemble yourself.

Back to our story: When I got back home that night, I was pleased to see a New York City network affiliate had done a brief story with video footage. Joy upon joys, the next day I discovered this centerfold in *The New York Daily News:*

Sounding Off
In Brass for
The Holidays

Upper center: My elbow on the right.   Bottom: Top of my head.
Note: I am not the reclining Prometheus in the bottom photograph.

Flash forward 24 years. (Yeah, in this context it may have been better to use a different word than "flash.") I returned to N.Y.C. to play in the 25th anniversary event. This time, my son Jonathan also played euphonium, our first father and son gig. On the way into the NBC studios to rehearse, we came across four men posing as the rock band *KISS*—in full regalia, makeup, and hair. Each man held a gleaming silver-plated tuba. The first true "heavy metal" band (and envy of us all.)

The Brass Player's Christmas Song
With apologies to Mel Torme...

Clarinets roasting on an open fire,
Jack Daniels-sipping as you watch,
Yuletide carols being played by brass choir,
And folks dressed up like a Sasquatch.

Everybody knows a trombone and some mistletoe,
Help to make the season bright.
Trumpeters with their bells all aglow,
Will find it hard to sleep tonight.

They know that Santa's on his way;
He's loaded lots of beer and munchies on his sleigh.
And every mother's child is going to spy,
To see if brassers really know how to fly.

And so I'm offering this simple phrase,
To kids from one to ninety-two,
Although its been said many times, many ways,
Brassy Christmas to you.

Unexpected Help

While I was a student at The King's College, I placed an ad in the Westchester County newspapers looking for brass players interested in joining a brass choir. I was shocked at the number of responses. A former horn player with the Cleveland Symphony, a Broadway trumpet player, and a trumpet player from the New York City Opera joined the group, which I called the *New World Brass Choir*. Almost every member of the group had more experience than I did, but they were very happy to have the chance to step out of the subordinate roles in their usual gigs to play in a brass choir.

At our first concert I was appalled to realize that some airhead (me) had forgotten to bring the mallet for the chimes. Good thing there was a thick handle on the kitchen knife I had packed to make my PB&J that day. The butt end of the knife actually produced a sound I preferred over the wooden mallet.

In the spring of 1977 we were hired by Maryknoll Seminary in Ossining, N.Y. to provide music for the 50th Anniversary celebration of Bishop James E. Walsh's priesthood. After the rehearsal, we sat on the lawn outside the church in order to enjoy the warm sunshine and beautiful landscaping. Birds twittered, butterflies flittered...

We hear a low thumping sound from inside the church. The thumps quickly turn into an orgy of irrhythmic pounding. Who is messing with the tympani? I spring to my feet and rush into the church, preparing to chew out the kid I expect to find flailing away on the kettle drums. It's Bishop Walsh! The Bishop gives me a sheepish grin and explains he has always wanted to play the kettle drums. What could I say but "Have fun!" It isn't often you get to make a bishop's dream come true.

One of my most unusal aural experiences came during the *Ithaca College Tuba-Euphonium Ensemble's* first concert at Ithaca College. One piece's final chord consisted of only the root and the fifth. The tuning was so perfect that we clearly heard the summation tone[13]—the third—eerily floating on top of the sound. We had never heard it in rehearsal, so it came as quite a surprise during the concert. Maybe it was the only time we were all really in tune?

***1812 Overture*, 3rd Trombone part (Outdoor concert)**

---

[13] The summation tone is created when the vibrations of two notes combine to form the pitch that is the sum of the two frequencies. This can also occur when a single brass player produces the low note with the lips and hums a higher note.

A Funny Thing Happened on the Way to the...

Q: What phrase is used most often by a trombonist at work?
A: "Would you like fries with that?"

There are so many underemployed musicians, more and more
graduate from music schools and conservatories every year, yet there
are fewer and fewer jobs available. The vast majority of us need to
find a variety of "day jobs" to support our music addiction.

Fortunately, I've never been so desperate as to work in a fast
food establishment. Unfortunately, I've been even more desperate: I
once took a job as a telemarketer, which I quit after one week. I
taught music in Schoharie for ten years, and then ran my one-man
water conditioning business, Schoharie Valley Water Systems, for
twenty-five years. (You thought I was kidding about "tubists" and
that plumbing thing?) I also taught as an adjunct professor at the
College of St. Rose and Hartwick College over a ten-year period. These
day jobs made for some frantic drives to get to my pit gigs on time.

One of the first things I learned to do was change clothes
while driving. It really isn't as dangerous and foolhardy as it sounds
when you consider that this was usually on a deserted Interstate
highway, the car was on cruise control, I never took my eyes off the
road, and I always kept at least one appendage on the wheel. Not
once did I put my shoes on inside out.

The closest I came to arriving late at a performance was, of all
things, the Gala Opening of the new $5 million Alice Busch Theater
at Glimmerglass Opera in 1987. Now I'm not normally quick to point
an accusatory finger at others, but...I had offered to give a ride to one
of my student assistants and her mother, and they were both still
getting ready when I stopped by to pick them up. I guess I should
have known better than to trust that two women would be ready on
time for their first night at the opera. What was supposed to have
been a 30-minute cushion with which to show them around the new
facility turned into a race against time.

I got pulled over for speeding by a New York State Trooper on
my way down that big hill on U.S. 20 near Cherry Valley. If he had
written me a ticket I would've been at least ten minutes late. There is
a very strict policy about that in the contract, including billing the
latecomer for expenses incurred by the Opera company if it chooses
to hold the curtain. International opera stars Frederica Von Stade
and Alan Titus probably get a fair amount of coin for overtime, there
were reviewers from major national and international publications,
and numerous luminaries were in the audience. Sweat poured down
my face as the officer got out of his car and strode toward me like the
Grim Reaper on a mission.

I rolled down my window and before the officer could say a word I wiped the sweat from my eyes, apologized for speeding, and explained I was late for a very important opening. If I didn't get there on time it could cause a lot of problems. I had already decided to go with the truth since it probably wouldn't work to ask one of the women to fake being in labor.

The officer grinned, and said, "I've never seen anyone look so guilty! I'll let you go, but you have to keep it to 55."

I just barely made it on time. As it turned out, there was at least one attendee who dropped in late.

The first half of the program consisted of a selection of arias and duets featuring the aforementioned international opera stars. The trombones were only invited to play on a few of these pieces, which led to the usual downtime. As we waited, principal trombonist Don Robertson noticed a spider spinning its own ringside seat amongst the tubing of his trombone slide. Don lifted his horn up to show us and the spider slowly rapelled to the floor, where he was greeted by the bottom of second trombonist Dan Martin's rapidly descending shoe. I told you there was a strict policy about lateness.

On the Road

Having had a family, it was a blessing the majority of my gigs were not "road shows." That said, I love to travel—and who doesn't like to combine pleasure with pleasure whenever possible?

I once played bass trombone for a Christian vocal group while I was still in high school. Details of the gig are very foggy in my memory, but not the ride back home from Allentown, PA. It was after midnight and the driver of the car wanted to show off how fast his souped up something-or-other could go. We were closing in on 110 miles per hour, *not* on an Interstate, when I dared ask him to back off. Figuring he would take a possibly prophetic vision seriously, I told him that I'd had a dream the previous night about dying in a car crash. It was a lie, but he slowed down so I feel no remorse. Besides, I had recently seen that Drivers' Education movie featuring the aftermath of horrific car crashes. I had no desire to embark on a film career, posthumously or otherwise.

Touring with The King's College Choir in the early 1970s was one of the best parts of my college education. This was the choir from Briarcliff Manor, N.Y., not the famous British men's choir by the same name. I played trombone in the oft-used brass ensemble and sang on the other numbers. The group toured the U.S. for a week and a half each spring and did many short weekend trips throughout the academic year.

One highlight was the impromptu singing of Mozart's "Ave Verum" in the National Cathedral in Washington, D.C. Afterward, our accompanist, Joan Dilley, asked if it might be possible to play their superb pipe organ. Since they knew she performed with the Billy Graham Crusade, permission was granted. We gathered around the console in eager anticipation. She played the first chord and burst into tears from the sheer joy of the sound. If you've never gone to an organ concert in such a space, go!

We traveled by bus and stayed with host families at each destination. Upon arrival, the guys got off the bus first in order to unload suitcases and equipment, then the ladies got off. (Insert your own joke here about how women get off on watching men work.) At one stop as I was the last guy off the bus, one of our hosts wise-cracked, "These must be all the King's men." Without missing a beat I loudly replied, "Yes, and all the King's horses will be out in a minute." The sopranos and altos were not amused. A couple of the tenors glared at me on behalf of the ladies, but who cares what tenors think?

As I mentioned earlier, I had been so fascinated with the flute part in *Chicago's* hit song "Colour My World" that I borrowed a flute and learned how to play it. My girlfriend, Barbara Bigger, was a flute major and member of the choir, so I often borrowed her flute to noodle[14] around. On one of the tours the choir performed J.S. Bach's "Sheep and Lambs May Safely Graze," accompanied by two flutes and organ. Unfortunately, Barb's back, injured in a previous accident, began acting up again. (Before I met her, she had fallen off a bed during a tickle fight. When the E.R. nurse looked askance, she said, "Oh, no, its OK; it was with another girl." This was the early 1970s, so either gender would have raised an eyebrow or two.) The host in whose home she stayed offered her some Darvon to relieve the pain. Evidently, the dosage was far too strong. She took a shower—without closing the shower curtain—and apparently was too drugged up to even attend the concert. Our conductor, Dr. Dean Arlton, was going to cut that number from the program, but since I had often noodled around on that piece I volunteered to fill in on the second part. With Cheryl Van Deusen's lovely tone on the top part, my breathy, thin tone was sufficiently masked to allow for an adequate performance. Flautists will be relieved to know it was the last time I played flute in public.

For several years in the 1980s, I had a seasonal gig playing euphonium and trombone with *The Deutschländers*, a German/American dance combo based out of Albany, N.Y. One season we were hired to play a weekend gig at a bar in Saranac Lake,

---

[14] "Noodle" is the musical term used for tooting on an instrument you know little about.

near Lake Placid, N.Y. This is Country & Western music territory; there was even a convenience store in the area with a sign that advertised "Gas, Groceries, Guns, & Guitars." The owner of the bar wanted to try to mix things up a little by putting on an Oktoberfest, complete with a roasted pig on the well-stocked buffet table. We arrived on Friday afternoon, checked in to their very basic motel next door, and played to an enthusiastic crowd of one—not counting the groupies, um, spouses we brought with us. The chagrined owner paid us off and sent us home the next morning. Too bad, the buffet was delicious!

At one *Deutschländers* appearance, an Oktoberfest in the Catskills, a New York City band preceded us on the bandstand, playing the traditional tunes in their own unique Ska style. I looked out over the crowd, expecting a sea of Hitler-like scowls, but the audience enjoyed their food and beer, clapping and toasting as if Ska was the original oompah. (Must have been strong beer!) Even the memory feels as surreal as an episode of *The Twilight Zone.*

My other sometime German band gig is with *The Katskill Danz Kapelle* out of Oneonta, N.Y. The band's leader, René Prins, inherited his father's European band library, including a lot of rare musical gems from the late 19th and early 20th centuries. It was with this group that I played on a moving train, pulled by an old steam locomotive on a run from Milford to Cooperstown, N.Y. René also conducts the Oneonta Town Band, where every concert we can count on performing at least one of those glad-you're-not-forgotten pieces from the early years of band literature.

I've played in the pit for two national tours of Broadway shows. I'll write more about *Man of La Mancha* elsewhere in this book. For the tour of *Ragtime* I played the tuba/euphonium book. What a treat! Fun music and a terrific show. The one oddity, besides there being a tuba/euphonium book, was that the actress playing the role of Mother had appeared in the original Broadway production. Several times during the run, the music director, in a voice oddly reminiscent of Anthony Perkins in *Psycho,* passed along notes provided by Mother. Evidently, Mother was not pleased with what she heard from the pit. What a Mother...

The longest tour I ever did was as principal euphonium with the International Symphonic Wind Orchestra in 1975. A summer in Scandinavia! It rained a bit the first day, and then we had an unending stretch of gorgeous, sunny days. We traveled by coach and ferry, and our accommodations alternated between hotels and host families arranged through the People to People organization.

One particularly memorable experience was my first—and only—trip to a nude beach. The host and his children disrobed and ran into the water; his wife and I did not. The beach was on the North Sea. The ch-ch-chilly North Sea. That infamous Seinfeld scene about "shrinkage" had not yet been written, but I was inhibited enough already without adding that well-known pressure to the mix.

Following our concert at the Vigeland Sculpture Park in Oslo, a woman came backstage and said, "Are you Frank Meredith?" Jean Heindel was a gym teacher at my high school alma mater and happened to be in Oslo for summer study. She went to the concert on a whim, saw my name, and wondered if I was related to Flo Meredith, her colleague and my stepmother. My colleagues in the band only heard the first part of the conversation, and I could see the wonder in their eyes at my having an audience member come looking for me. That was a nice ego boost. Speaking of ego boosts...

Our principal horn player, Dennis Cohen, told me he liked my euphonium tone so much that he had been trying to emulate it. Since he was a graduate of the Curtis Institute of Music who had studied with members of the Philadelphia Orchestra, I took it as a great compliment.

In Copenhagen I stayed with a euphonium player in the Danish Army band. I'll never forget his howls of laughter when he tried to get me to say the equivalent of "red strawberries with cream on": *Rød grød med fløde på.*[15] How *do* they make those vowel sounds?

As we prepared to depart from a stop in Denmark, one of our oboists, Patti Thayer, was the only no-show for the bus. There was no answer to a phone call to the host's house. Since Patti and I had become close friends, I volunteered to stay behind and figure out a way for us to catch up with the bus later. To this day I have no idea how I would have accomplished that. I had no credit card (back in the days when you had to have a good-paying job to get one), little cash, there were no such things as ATMs or cell phones, and my Danish language skills were limited to, "Thanks for the meal," "I love you," and a hilarious version of *Rød grød med fløde på.* (I understand this limited vocabulary will still get you pretty far in Denmark today.)

As it turned out, Patti's host had given her a ride to the next destination. Someone aware of the situation drove up and offered me a ride. Good thing, because my next best option would have been to look for a car heading in the right direction, tell the driver I love her, point to the town on a map, and tell her how urgently I needed to get there for some red strawberries and cream.

My host in Stockholm was Gunnar Mellin, the Swedish equivalent of Cliff Barrows, a well-known bass soloist with the Billy Graham crusade. The breakfasts he served included weak beer, curdled milk, and open-faced sandwiches. I later met up with him in New York City on one of his trips to sing in the U.S.

---

[15] Here is a link to a YouTube video where you can hear this for yourself. www.youtube.com/watch?v=z8VziyktyS0&noredirect=1

Being raised in a family of seven, our food was always prepared unsalted so we could each season the food as we liked. During one homestay in Aarhus, Denmark, I immediately reached for the salt and sprinkled it on the potatoes, veggies, and meat. The wife burst into tears and left the table. The children stared at me in horror. I double-checked to make sure it was salt I had used and not sugar. The host gently explained that it was the cook's responsibility to season the food properly so that everyone would be pleased. To taste the food, then add salt to it, would be the same as saying the cook was not very good. To salt the food without even tasting it was a slap in the face. I quickly apologized and explained why I had done that. All was forgiven. But they did make me try to say "red strawberries with cream on" more times than I thought necessary.

Traveling leaves little time for practicing, and playing concerts does not provide enough "face time" with the instrument to keep in top shape. During a day off, a few of us got together to play some brass quintets someone had wisely brought along. It was my first exposure to Viktor Ewald's *Brass Quintet No. 1,* one of the finest pieces of chamber music ever written. I also had the joy of joining in some woodwind quintet pieces, playing the horn part on euphonium.

This trip also introduced me to open-air museums with our visit to Stockholm's Skansen, the world's first museum to transport several dozen centuries-old buildings to one location, furnish them, and provide reenactors to recreate the crafts and lifestyles of the original inhabitants. I loved to imagine myself actually living in those buildings centuries ago. Since then I've been to a dozen more open-air museums in seven other countries.

One evening, Patti and I missed the last train out of Stockholm to our hosts' homes in the suburbs. We sat by the water, chatted, and watched the sunrise around 2:00 AM. I have no recollection of what we talked about, but I remember feeling like it was the best night of the trip.

Sidenote: In one of those "small world" coincidences, Patti and I haven't been in touch since 1975, but earlier this week I discovered that the brass quintet music I wanted to order was arranged by one of her twin sons, Christian McIvor, who went to college with Aaron Clermont, the tuba player in our brass quintet and husband of my son's ex-girlfriend. (No, you don't need to memorize that for the test at the end of the book.)

Following an outdoor concert in Stockholm, a young American woman came up to us, her face streaked with tears. Our closing number, "American Civil War Fantasy," made her so homesick that she just had to talk to some Americans. Such is the power of music.

As much fun as it is to travel, Dorothy was right when she said, "There's no place like home." Or as they say in Danish, *"Der er ikke noget sted som hjem."* I bet I could've pronounced that.

Food for Thought

This list was inspired when I heard a passage of flute music in parallel thirds, "tutti flutti." I'm no chef, so feel free to whip up your own recipes that might fit these titles.

Tutti Frutti Flutti

Tempo Primavera

Pesto Presto

Largo Escargot

Andante al Dente

Allegretto Spaghetto

Pizzicato Pizza

Grave Gravy

Forte Torte

Piano Torte

Pianissimo Panini

Vivace Carpaccio

Maestro Minestrone

Calamato Moderato

Trumpet Crumpets

Horn o' Polenta

Trombone T-bone

Tuba Macaroni

Piccolo Picante

Tympani Tempura

Moderato Marinara

Score Keepers

I like to think of conductors as "score keepers," men and women who "know the score" and seek to deliver a performance that is faithful to the composer's original intentions—although a judicious amount of personal interpretation may be allowed. In pursuit of my graduate studies in conducting, I chose to accept Ithaca College's offer of a graduate assistantship with their highly regarded orchestra conductor, Pamela Gearhart. Sadly, once I got to Ithaca I found out that Ms. Gearhart's idea of a graduate assistant was someone to set up the chairs at the rehearsals. I appealed to the Dean of the Music School and was reassigned to run a studio to tutor her conducting students. The entire year, she sent none of her students to see me. The only contact I ever had with Ms. Gearhart turned out to be that initial meeting in which I was told about the chairs. Fortunately, the Music School's iconic band director, Ed Gobrecht, took me under his wing. I learned more about musicianship and conducting from him than from any other teacher or conductor I've ever had. Coincidentally, his father was my father's trombone teacher, and Ed taught my stepmother, Flo Meredith, to play the glockenspiel.[16]

Besides being a consummate musician, Charles Schneider is one of the best and certainly the most influential "score keeper" for whom I have worked. In September 1978 the Catskill Symphony performed a concert at Schoharie High School. Following the performance I introduced myself to Maestro Schneider, told him I was new to the area, and asked him to let me know if he ever needed a bass trombone player. He did. I auditioned, got the job, and have played with that orchestra ever since. Chuck conducted the Utica Symphony and was the founding Music Director of Glimmerglass Opera, so I was soon invited to play with them, as well. Later he hired me to play with the Orpheus Theater in Oneonta, sub with the Schenectady Symphony, and play numerous other free-lance gigs. So there you have it. Chuck is ultimately to blame for casting me into a life in the pits.

I've studied conducting with several outstanding conductors, I have more than twenty-five years of conducting experience, and I've taught conducting at the college and graduate school levels, so I tend to be a bit unforgiving if the person conducting me is not up to the standards I would expect for the occasion. My complaints generally focus on four things: unclear conducting gestures, inefficient use of rehearsal time, rudeness toward the musicians, and poor knowledge or interpretation of the score.

Back in the 1990s I did a gig with Marvin Hamlisch. His music was very enjoyable, he was very personable, and he entertained us with his performance on the melodica.[17] In 2009 I played a second gig with him, but this time he conducted from the piano. He was not very personable. Oftentimes he was very unclear with his gestures and head nods, which inevitably led to rehearsal problems, after which he castigated the orchestra. I still enjoyed his music, but I did not enjoy working with him this time.

---

[16] Glockenspiel is German for "Dang, that thing is so loud it hurts my glockens!"

[17] A handheld, two-and-a-half octave reed organ. The performer blows into the instrument and plays the keyboard with one hand.

At Glimmerglass Opera in 2000, John Demain conducted the revival of John Phillip Sousa's operetta, *The Glass Blowers*. There were difficulties from the first rehearsal through the first performance. Evidently, there was no original full score, so our parts were repeatedly revised as the director worked out the staging and everyone tried to discern Sousa's original intentions. Maestro Demain seemed ill-prepared to me, we often had trouble following him, and he was a bit brusque with the orchestra. I never did warm up to him.

Therefore, I was not pleased to hear that he had been selected to conduct our 2012 production of *The Music Man*; but I'm very happy to relate that this time, working with Maestro Demain was a delightful experience. He had a wonderful rapport with the musicians and he did an outstanding job conducting. He also told us about his project to develop a Full Score[18] for every Rodgers and Hammerstein musical.

Traditionally, the conductor's score for most Broadway shows is what is called a Piano Score, meaning that all of the parts for the pit orchestra have been reduced to a two-line staff playable by a piano,[19] plus a separate line of music for the vocal parts. Typically, the composer of the musical gives the lyrics and a piano part to an orchestrator, who then writes out parts for the pit orchestra. The orchestrator often adds counter-melodies and usually has the freedom to flesh out the harmonies a bit. A Piano Score is developed from this and, if the conductor is lucky, some notations are added to give some indication of which notes the various instruments have been assigned. If the conductor is *very* lucky, a third line of music is added, giving more detail. Then the show goes into production. During the rehearsal process, numerous changes are made to the music. The number of instruments in the pit may change. In future productions, more changes are made. As a result, developing a Full Score from these various editions can be a daunting task, even under the best conditions.

Mr. Demain told us about the time he worked with a theater company in preparation for a 25th-Anniversary performance of Leonard Bernstein and Stephen Sondheim's *West Side Story*.[20] Not long after Mr. Bernstein began his first rehearsal with the group, he stopped the music, turned to Mr. Demain, and referring to the score said, "How the *&%#!^$@$ does anyone conduct from this thing!" A Full Score has since been produced.

---

[18] A score with an individual line showing the music for every instrument or voice.

[19] Sometimes this would require a lot more than ten fingers!

[20] The best Broadway show yet written. There can be no debate on this point.

Kristen Blodgette conducted the 2011 production of *Annie Get Your Gun* at Glimmerglass.[21] Ms. Blodgette has a long list of Broadway and International credits and is the music supervisor for all North American productions of Andrew Lloyd Weber's musicals, so I looked forward to learning from her as we began rehearsals. Much to my surprise, we did not get off to a good start. Many times we were asked to repeat a section, up to three times in a row, but we were not told why. It is expected for the conductor to tell the musicians what needs to be performed differently before repeating a section, so it felt to me as though we were wasting time as we had no idea if we were supposed to try to "fix" anything. I had also expected rehearsals to run even more efficiently than usual, since Broadway shows rarely have the luxury of adequate rehearsal time. If it is a touring show, they barely have enough time to play through all of the music once with the local musicians before each opening night. And then some of my colleagues were miffed at the start of several of the performances when sheets of paper listing additional conductor's comments and instructions appeared on our stands, but I thought that was a useful, time-saving device.

Again, I am very happy to say that my first impressions were wrong. I thoroughly enjoyed the run and the opportunity to work with and learn from Ms. Blodgette. Her conducting was clear and easy to follow, she showed real enthusiasm for the production, and she brought new life to the well-known show tunes.

As it turned out, my son, Nathan, has also worked with her. At the time of this writing (June 2014), he is nearing completion of a year-long tour as a sound engineer for the national tour of *Evita*, supervised by Kristen Blodgette.

And speaking of sons and score-keeping...

My son, Jonathan, and I took part in a tuba and euphonium festival at the Royal Northern College of Music in Manchester, England in 1999. As part of the event, we joined a large ensemble of tubas and euphoniums, performing a concert that was broadcast live on the BBC. One of the pieces had no key signature, so during the rehearsal I reminded Jonathan to watch out for the B-naturals, fearing he might play the much more common B-flat by mistake. Oh, foolish father! I should have known my son wouldn't make such a mistake. Just as I should have known that when we came upon the first B-natural during the concert, I would be the one to play B-flat.

Good thing no one else is keeping score.

---

[21] A classic Broadway musical performed with an orchestra of more than forty musicians is now part of every season's Glimmerglass lineup—a rarity in the age of synthesizers and smaller pit orchestras.

Union regulations require low brass players to employ toilet humor in all publications.

Read 'em and Weep

I've always been intrigued by the accounts I've read of the impact of John Phillip Sousa's band tours in the late 19th and early 20th centuries. In the days before recordings and radio, it was a major event to have a world-renowned band come to your town to play a concert, featuring performances by one or more of the world's leading instrumental or vocal soloists. Some of the music was so moving, grown men wept openly. One might ask, "What would it take to see such a response today?"

Well, since inquiring readers want to know...

In March of 1985 I underwent knee surgery for an injury sustained in a faculty basketball game. It took a heavy dose of painkillers to manage the resulting "discomfort." That same week, I was scheduled to play Mahler's *Symphony No. 1* with the Catskill Symphony. No way was I going to miss that! So, I loaded up on painkillers, my wife loaded me into the car, and then she delivered me to the concert hall. I think I played well; at least, I don't recall cooking up any clams. I do vividly remember playing the last page of music, though. Tears streamed down my face at the sheer beauty of the sounds that surrounded me.[22] Or was it the painkillers? I just watched the video link below. It wasn't the painkillers.

It is not uncommon to hear sniffles from the audience when performing such Broadway shows as *Les Miserables, Miss Saigon,* and *Man of La Mancha.* I get choked up when I play for them. And then there are the death scenes in many operas, such as *La Boheme.* My next three productions are all tearjerkers: I'm currently playing in the Glimerglass pit for *Madame Butterfly* and *Carousel,* and then I will be the stage director and play in the pit for the musical *Chess,* the ending of which will "out Puccini Puccini." (I'm buying stock in *Kleenex* now.)

This next story may seem to be a *non sequitur,* but it is not. It is the reason for the other half of the section title.

Reading is a popular pastime many pit musicians enjoy to while away the tacets. When this takes place in a pit, there is little chance anyone in the audience will notice. However, when confronted with a tacet movement while on stage with an orchestra, one must keep the reading material hidden on the music stand so as not to appear disinterested in the goings on aroud them.

In many concerts, there will be an entire piece that does not employ all of the instruments. If it is a long piece, those players leave the stage. If the piece is only several minutes in duration, those players will usually remain in their seats. I have learned that it is wise to determine who is leaving the stage—and when—*before* the concert.

About twenty years ago during a Utica Symphony concert, we came to a piece in the program that did not include the trombones. I had been looking forward to that piece because I was in the middle of some book or other and was eager to get back to the story. So eager, that I didn't notice that the rest of the brass section left the stage. My head was buried in the book while the rest of the orchestra proceeded to play. Evidently, some audience members wondered why a trombone player sat in the back row all by himself, staring at his music stand but never playing a note.

I sent Maestro Schneider a written apology. I can't believe I was so oblivious! It's almost enough to make a grown man weep.

---

[22]YouTube video of the final three minutes of Mahler's *Symphony No. 1.*
https://www.youtube.com/watch?v=LdF97F84JME

How Can I Miss You If You Won't Go Away?

Volume is far and away the biggest complaint all pit musicians hear, especially if the venue has no pit in which to bury the sound. (Insert your own dead musician joke here.) Brass players, percussionists, and anyone playing something electronic are often handed tickets for noise violations on their way into the pit.

I've been in pits where they've draped heavy curtains or added layers of padding to help muffle the sound. Now I certainly understand the need to hear the singers and dialogue on stage, but muting a dance performance? Sad, but true.

Brass players in a pit often need a variety of mutes to alter and muffle the sound. Snare drum parts are sometimes played using one's fingertips. Unfortunately, there's not much you can do with a high flute or piccolo part, unless you give it to the synthesizer.

During one Glimmerglass rehearsal, a guest conductor kept giving me the "Naypalm"—trombonist Hal Reynolds' term for the palm down gesture the conductor shows for less volume. It was a passage where I was the only trombone with a part to play, doubling the low reeds and strings. I kept getting the Naypalm, even though I could barely hear myself play. So I held my instrument up, moved the slide, but played nothing. The conductor beamed with pleasure and nodded at me. I continued the charade for the first couple of performances, then didn't even bother taking my horn off its stand. As often as I've told this story, it suddenly occurs to me that somewhere there is a conductor who brags to his colleagues about the time he managed to get a bass trombone player to play softly.

One summer I played a gig with the Tonawanda American Legion Band for a national competition in Boston. The conductor, Herb Ludwig, told this story about a young percussionist's initiation to the band: The youngster had been assigned to play the bass drum part, which he carefully scanned in preparation. His eyes fell upon something he had not seen before—a measure of rest with the letters G.P. printed boldly above it. He asked the section leader what it meant. ("Grand Pause"—the entire group is *silent*.) The leader said, "Oh, that means Great Pound; it's a bass drum solo. When we get there, make sure you hit the drum as hard as you can. Really impress us." And so he did, nearly causing several coronaries.

Brass players employ a variety of mutes, both to soften the sound and change the tone color. Each mute has an arrangement of cork around the upper rim which is supposed to hold the mute in place, if you jam it up the bell far enough. Of course, Murphy's Law sees to it that during a random quiet passage, the Law of Gravity will overcome the friction established between the cork and the instrument bell. The mute will drop to the floor, rattle around, then drop down to the next level of risers as it seeks to make good its escape.

Sometimes the orchestrator for a show seems to take sadistic delight in calling for impossibly quick mute changes. Even if we manage to effect the change, the new mute might make a clanging sound as it is inserted or the old mute might clatter to the floor. One alternative is to quickly jam the old mute between our knees, but that takes additional skill to avoid self-mutilation. Nobody wants to have to explain *that* injury at a worker's compensation hearing.

My freshman year in college I was one of three new trombone majors. The other two, Paula and Tony, walked into our first band rehearsal and stared daggers at each other. They had met before. And it was all about the mutes...

They had been selected as the first two chairs in New York's 1970 All-State Band, conducted by the legendary William Revelli, an old school, drill sergeant style of conductor. Evidently, one of the pieces on the program required mutes, and Dr. Revelli made it tyrannically clear that he did not want to hear a single mute clang against an instrument bell during the transfer. At the dress rehearsal, Paula, who was sitting second chair to Tony's first, managed to insert her mute quietly, but when she lifted the horn into position her mute slid out and clattered to the floor. Dr. Revelli cut off the band and glared furiously at the trombones. In fear, Paula turned and looked at Tony. Dr. Revelli presumed by that action that it was Tony's mute that had fallen, so he immediately demoted Tony to second chair and moved Paula to first. No one dared to utter a word of correction to this maestro.

Happily, Tony and Paula became good friends in college—and I became a euphonium major. My small bore tenor trombone was no match for the big sounds they produced on their larger horns with an F-attachment. Besides, euphonium mutes are rarely used, and when they are, the euphonium's bell points upward so there is no danger of the mute falling out.

Collection of Collectives

If you can have a "murder of crows" and an "exaltation of larks," why aren't there collective nouns for musicians? Here are my proposals:

A Twitter of Piccolos
A Champagne of Flutes
A Seduction of Oboes
A Reverie of English Horns
A Fountain of Clarinets
A Priesthood of Alto Clarinets
An Intrigue of Bass Clarinets
A Forest of Bassoons
An Abyss of Contrabassoons
A Cackle of Soprano Saxophones
An Undulation of Alto Saxophones
A Smolder of Tenor Saxophones
A Grumble of Baritone Saxophones
A Pinch of Piccolo Trumpets
A Brace of Trumpets
A Snuggle of Flugelhorns
A Party of Horns
A Triumph of Trombones
An Audacity of Bass Trombones
A Honeycomb of Euphoniums
A Cannonade of Tubas
An Aristocracy of Violins
A Tryst of Violas
A Contemplation of Cellos
A Phalanx of Double Basses
A Chatter of Snare Drums
A Kettle of Tympani
A Skeleton of Xylophones
An Exclamation of Cymbals
A Wave of Suspended Cymbals
A Eureka of Triangles

A Shiver of Maracas
A Sparkle of Celestas
A Cord *(sic)* of Pianos
A Phantom of Organs
An Effervescence of Harpsichords
A Halo of Harps
A Flirtation of Guitars
A Romance of Lutes
An Envy of Theorbos
A Frolic of Banjos
A Señora of Accordions
A Swarm of Harmonicas
A Grate of Kazoos
A Subtlety of Bagpipes
A Yodel of Alphorns
A Compliment *(sic)* of Sopranos
A Bouquet of Altos
A Pride of Tenors
A Beard of Basses
A Vacancy of Castratos
A Lair of Conductors

Cuckoo for Koko

Back in its formative years, Glimmerglass Opera performed in the auditorium of Cooperstown High School. The biggest perk for the orchestra was that the pit, as is typical in most school auditoriums, was on the same level as the house seats, affording a great view of the stage. And since the bass trombone has so many tacet passages, I had a great seat to enjoy the show.

My favorite operetta, hands down, is *The Mikado*, by Gilbert and Sullivan—wonderful music, witty dialogue, and many classic comedic roles. It even pokes fun at the disguise of one of the lead characters, who masquerades as the second trombone in the Titipu town band. We were blessed to have veteran Broadway and movie actor, Alan Kass, to star in the leading role of Koko, providing the funniest moments I have thus far seen on any stage.

There is a scene where the hapless Koko, in order to save his head from the executioner's axe (or be boiled in oil), must woo and win the fearsome Katisha, whose right elbow is so attractive that men come from miles around to admire it. Katisha is often played by a "generously proportioned" alto and is costumed to look even larger. Her face is made up to look like something from a horror movie.

So each night when our Koko uttered his words of woodom, his face and body contorted in the vain attempt to hide his disgust. At the climax of his romantic overture, he can bear it no longer. He turns, flees, and climbs the garden trellis, hoping to escape his fate; but halfway up the trellis he freezes. In that moment, we know he realizes his failure to win Katisha will seal his doom. But are there fates worse than death?

Koko clings to the trellis with one hand, reaches plantively with the other toward the imposing bulk of Katsiha, and cries, "Shrink not from me!...(He slinks back to her.) True it is that under a poor mask of *disgust*, I have endeavored to conceal a passion whose inner fires are *broiling* the soul within me...Katisha! I dare not hope for your love, but *I will not live without it!*"

The above description doesn't begin to do justice to the comedic genius of Alan Kass. You need to understand that in every single performance, he found different nuances, expressions, and timing to mine every bit of humor from the absurd situation. We in the pit knew the lines as well as he did, anticipated what was coming next, and were enthralled and delighted by each night's variations. Fortunately, the audience also convulsed with laughter, because we needed the time to recover before we had to play the next song.

Let Me Rephrase That!

In 1985 I was hired to play euphonium with the Albany Symphony for the premier performance and recording of George Lloyd's *Symphony No. 11*.[23] The euphonium is my favorite instrument and, as I previously mentioned, there are only a handful of instances where it is used in an orchestral composition. So to have a new symphony with an actual euphonium part was unheard of—and to my knowledge, it is still the only symphony with a significant euphonium part throughout the piece.

I eagerly anticipated the first rehearsal. My part was all prepared, especially the soloistic passages. I couldn't wait for the rest of the orchestra to discover the beauty and richness that a euphonium can add to the sound palette. I had even recently purchased a Swiss-made Willson euphonium, noted for its superior tone quality. Up to that point, all of my playing with the instrument had been done with band or piano accompaniment. I had learned to make the necessary pitch adjustments to play in tune in those

---

[23] Recording available from Albany Records.   Audio of the first movement: https://www.youtube.com/watch?v=dAnFyzowTfU

situations; however, playing with an orchestra proved to be quite a challenge. I'd already had seven years' experience as an orchestral bass trombone player, yet the euphonium was an entirely different beast. I left the rehearsal shaken and frustrated.

It was after 11:00 PM by the time I got home. I rushed to the phone to call my colleague, Dave Unland, tuba/euphonium professor at Ithaca College. Surely, he could help me figure out what was going on. My frustration grew as the phone rang and rang. It never occurred to me that he might have already gone to bed. As I was about to hang up, he finally answered. I thought he would recognize my voice so I didn't take the time to identify myself, blurting, "I'm about to slit my wrists!"

Poor, groggy Dave. He thought he was getting a call from a suicidal student! When we finally calmed each other down, I wound up deciding to use a Yamaha euphonium for the gig. It didn't have the same tone quality, but it was much easier to play in tune.

Why Don't They IMAX the Dancers?

Ballet is the one genre I wish I could perform far more often. The orchestra is an equal partner in communicating the emotional impact of the story, and we almost never get complaints that we are too loud. The dozen-year span I played *The Nutcracker* with the Mohawk Valley Ballet and Utica Symphony is among my top ten career highlights. The week-long run of performances always sold out the 3,200-seat Stanley Performing Arts Center in Utica, N.Y. The ballet company hired professionals for the lead dancers, but the *corps de ballet* consisted of young amateurs from the region. It always amazed us in the pit that the children we saw backstage were the same mature-looking dancers we saw on stage.

For the "Dance of the Snowflakes," a large cylindrical cage filled with shredded newspaper rotated above the stage, releasing fluttering scraps of newsprint. Invariably, stray "flakes" found their way into the tuba bell and any unsuspecting brass player's mouthpiece. More than once I lifted my instrument to play and had to scramble to clear the "snow" before playing. Each year when we opened our music for the first rehearsal, we uncovered hibernating snowflakes from the previous season.

The Act Two curtain opened to reveal the Land of Sweets shrouded in ground fog. Of course, the carbon dioxide fog rolled off the stage and into the pit, obscured the music, and gagged the woodwind and brass players as we tried to breathe enough air to play the long phrases.

Sadly, this gig ended when the ballet company stopped hiring the orchestra in favor of using a recording. I understand the economic wisdom, especially since they still sell out every performance, but what a shame the audience misses out on the richness of sound that only a live orchestra can provide.

Several years later, Betsy and I took our sons and their girlfriends to see the Pennsylvania Ballet's *Nutcracker* in Philadelphia. I had very much enjoyed working at Glimmerglass in 2005 with their conductor, Beatrice Jona Affron, and I couldn't wait to luxuriate in Tchaikovsky's music in the famous Academy of Music, but it was not to be: they used a recording! And their sound system was nothing special. I never would have gone to that expense if I had known in advance that there would be no orchestra. I'd much rather watch video-recorded dancers on an IMAX screen accompanied by a live orchestra. Doesn't that make far more sense, artistically?

TCB with the KGB

One of my favorite ballet experiences was the time I played for the *Glasnost Ballet* during their U.S. tour in 1987, the year before the fall of the Berlin Wall. Stars of the *Kirov* and *Mariinsky* ballet companies joined other outstanding Russian dancers in an evening of ballet highlights.

During rehearsal, I noticed that two somber men in suits observed from just offstage. I wisecracked to no one in particular, "They look like KGB!"

Both men's eyes suddenly met mine; I have no idea how they heard me from that distance. My look of surprise (and nervousness?) must have convinced them that I posed no threat of any kind. I don't *know* that they were KGB, but...

From that point on I took care of business (TCB) and avoided any further wisecracks.

Family Ties

While completing my Master's in Brass Performance at Ithaca College in the summer of 1978, I had the pleasure of studying with Allen Ostrander, the "Father of Bass Trombone." His career included playing for the legendary Arturo Toscanini in the NBC Symphony (imagine a network today sponsoring an orchestra?) and in the New York Philharmonic. Allen's excellent method books and transcriptions are used worldwide. And we once played a gig together.

I've been the bass trombonist in the Catskill Symphony since 1978. During one concert series back in the 1980s, the program only included one piece with parts for trombones. The rest of the section called for subs in order to play other engagements, so Maestro Schneider asked me if I'd like to move up and play Principal. It was just the one piece and not a long one at that. The catch: it was written in alto clef and, of course, in that range. Did I have a tenor or alto trombone to use? Not any more, but would it be alright if I played it on the bass trombone? Maestro Schneider gave his assent. I prepared the part. I had no problem with the clef, thanks to all those hours spent hacking away at the Blazhevich "Clef Studies," so I strode confidently into the first rehearsal. By now you've probably guessed who was hired to fill my spot on bass trombone: Allen Ostrander. It is exceedingly rare to have two bass trombones at the same gig. (Some say there are any number of good, nonmusical reasons for this, but they're obviously just jealous of the larger slide and bell.) Allen took one look at me sitting in the principal's chair with the alto trombone part in front of me and a bass trombone in my hand, shook his head, and laughed. The gig went well, and I think I am safe in saying I am one of the very few bass trombonists to play on the same gig with Papa Ostrander—and the only one to do so covering an alto part.

"THE BLUENOTES"

"Music As You Like It"

For Booking Information—Write, Wire or Call

Beryl D. Stauffer, Mgr.   Robert J. Meredith
                                              Leader
520 Baer Avenue   213 Fulton Street
Hanover, Pa.   Hanover, Pa.
Phone 2-7258   Phone 7-2685

Our Repertoire Includes The Finest In Swing, Fox Trots, Mambos, Calyspos, Dixieland, Standard And Pop Tunes, For Dining, Listening And Dancing.

The Blue Notes, *Robert Meredith, trombone. (c. 1956)*

I have the trombones my father (Robert Meredith Sr.) and my uncle (Frank Neail) played, waiting to be passed on to the first of my grandchildren who wants to carry on the family tradition. (I have five grandsons, as of this writing, and a sixth grandchild on the way.)

My father was an accomplished trombonist and arranger. Our first gig together was in May of 1961, when as a 7-year-old I carried flowers at the front of the *Lyric Band* during the local Memorial Day parade.[24] As a teen, I joined my father in the trombone section of that band.

His father was a pianist and sometime composer, in addition to his long career as editor-in-chief of the local newspaper. We have a framed copy of his published song, "Hail to Elkdom."

My great-grandfather and great-great-grandfather were both preachers and musicians. My brother Dan, a very talented singer-songwriter,[25] high school choir director, and finalist for Teacher-of-the-Year in Pennsylvania, has the 1854 melodeon our ancestors used in their ministries. I suspect the "pit" those 19th century ministers preached about is more horrendous than any I've been in (so far.)

As a parent, there is no greater joy than seeing your son or daughter succeed in life. So it has been a special delight that I've been able to share pit experiences with all three of my sons. My oldest son, Christopher, also plays bass trombone. During his junior year in high school (1999) we were both hired to sub with the Schenectady Symphony Orchestra. In 2000 I was able to pass to him a call I got to play in the pit for *Anything Goes* with the Orpheus Theater. And in 2001 when I played the lead on stage for *Man of La Mancha,* he returned from Ithaca College to play in the pit.

---

[24] See photograph on page vii.

[25] You can download his music for free at www.SDGministry.com

Several years ago, when Christopher played a concert series with the Mississippi Symphony in Jackson, the substitute principal trombone player introduced himself: Doug Mark. When Christopher told him his name, Doug said, "Meredith? That's funny. I just left my position with the Utica Symphony, and the bass trombonist there is named Meredith, too."

Jonathan is a high school choir director and has directed more than a dozen musicals throughout the region. My wife and I have played in the pit under his outstanding direction several times already. He won a TANYS award as Music Director in the production of *Man of La Mancha* that I directed in 2012 (more on that later.) In 2013, his was the first high school licensed to perform *Spamalot*. Of course I wore the Killer Rabbit slippers I had gotten for Father's Day, much to the delight of children in the front row.

Nathan is currently touring as an audio tech with the Broadway show *Evita* and will tour with *Pippin* in 2014-15. Our first pit experience together was playing at Schenectady Light Opera for *Gypsy* in 2004, which featured his trumpet calls in the show stopping number, "Gotta Get a Gimmick." He has gone on to music direct several shows, including a production of *Les Miserables* at Schenectady Light Opera in which he brought out nuances in the music I had never heard in the seven previous professional and Broadway productions I have seen.

Two of my boys, playing nicely together at last.
Nathan and Jonathan Meredith in the pit of Les Miserables.
Schenectady Light Opera, May 2012

You Might Be a Pit Musician

Comedian Jeff Foxworthy is well known for his "You might be a Redneck" jokes. If he were a pit musician, maybe he would say:

If half of the clothes in your closet are black, and you aren't a priest or nun...you might be a pit musician.

If you don't mind flying in coach because the seat is roomier than your workspace...

If you can identify at least three species of centipedes...

If you keep a change of clothes in your gig bag...

If you own your own music stand light...

If you know the lyrics and dialogue for an entire Broadway musical...

If you have named the mouse that lives in the wall behind your chair...

If you have memorized most of your music simply because you've played it so many days in a row...

If you know what V.S.[26] means at the bottom of the page...

If you have considered buying night vision goggles to help read your music...

If you know the best way to remove squashed spiders and moths from your music...

If your car has its own mailing address...

If you know what Tams-Witmark's music books smell like...

If you know exactly how many pages you can read before your next entrance...

If they mic your instrument so they can make you sound softer in the final mix...

If you frequently hear lots of singing from one floor up and you aren't in your apartment...

If there are autograph seekers waiting outside the stage door, but not for you...

If you've ever worn a T-shirt with a tux imprint to a gig...you might be a *Redneck* pit musician.

---

[26] *Volti Subito* is Italian for "turn suddenly."

Como Cuomo?

In June of 1993 I played tenor trombone in the free-lance brass ensemble hired to play for the wedding of Matilda Cuomo, daughter of then-Governor of New York, Mario Cuomo. The ceremony was held in the Cathedral of the Immaculate Conception in Albany, next to the Governor's Mansion. Due to the high profile attendees, including politicians and celebrities such as Larry King, the State Police did a thorough security scan of the facility while we rehearsed a few hours before the wedding. I found it odd that they never came up onto the altar to check out the musicians and our cases, etc. Having read hundreds of murder mysteries over the years, many while counting rests during long breaks in rehearsals, my mind chewed on the plot possibilities of a crafty international assassin disguised as a brass player, and how the dastardly deed could be accomplished with a hidden blow dart incorporated into the brass instrument. (I may still write that book, stay tuned. It could be part of a series, one of which will be about a pit musician who murders the maestro during an opera performance.)

The bride was attended by a party of twenty-four, all relatives of the bride or groom. Larry King remarked that the wedding gown was, "The longest dress I have ever seen in my life." Needless to say, the time it took for the bride and her dress to get down the aisle made it the longest processional I've ever played. I rarely played tenor trombone any more, so my chops were in desperate straits by the end of it. Perhaps that was a contributing factor in the thoughts of secret assassins?

I don't recall anything else about the wedding, but I was again tempted to mischief when the check for the gig arrived in the mail. I was very surprised to see that it was "signed" by Mario Cuomo. I had not been in favor of many of Governor Cuomo's political policies or the effect they had on my one-man water conditioning business. Rush Limbaugh had often taken jabs at the Governor, especially during his coyness over the possibility of launching a run for the Presidency in the 1992 election. Therefore, I briefly considered endorsing the check over to Mr. Limbaugh, hoping Mr. Cuomo would notice and feel some measure of annoyance. But the likelihood he would notice was virtually nil, and even though Mr. Limbaugh would no doubt have been greatly amused, it wasn't worth losing out on the $80.00. Besides, I figured the money would be much better spent in the research of clandestine blow dart techniques.

Surprise Endings

When you read my short stories at the end of this book, you will see that I love surprise endings. The "longest" surprise ending I've experienced came as a result of our production of Sigmund Romberg's *The Student Prince* at Glimmerglass in 1984. This was when the opera company still performed in the auditorium at Cooperstown High School, so I had an excellent view of the stage whenever I wasn't playing. This turns out to be a key element in the story, as you will see.

The operetta is about Prince Karl Franz, heir to the throne of the mythical kingdom of Karlsberg. He is sent to Heidelberg incognito as an ordinary student for an education and to improve his social skills. The first social skill he learns is how to fall in love with a commoner—a tavern keeper's niece named Kathie—even though he has been promised in marriage to Princess Margaret ever since they were children. He serenades Kathie with the beautiful song, "Deep in My Heart, Dear."

By the end of the first Act; in the classic boy-meets-girl, boy-loses-girl, boy-gets-girl format; Prince Karl receives a surprise visit from Princess Margaret and her mother, who tell him the King is ill and the Prince has been ordered to return home. Karl Franz and Kathie consider an elopement, but he decides he must obey and fulfill his duty. He promises Kathie he will soon return, then goes home.

During the intermission, two years pass—they must have racked up quite a lot of sales at the concession stands in the lobby. Karl Franz is now the King, and the time has come for him to marry Margaret, even though he loves Kathie and Margaret is frequently out on "secret maneuvers" with Captain Tarnitz.

As fate would have it, one of Karl Franz's Heidelberg friends dies, and the King is persuaded to return to the college town for a reunion with his drinking buddies. What could go wrong?

Princess Margaret gets there ahead of him, finds Kathie, and talks her into rejecting the King for the good of the kingdom. Besides, Margaret has decided she loves Karl Franz after all and, being a princess, she has never been good at sharing.

Karl Franz finally arrives and meets with Kathie. She lies by telling him that since he hasn't been around for these past two years, she has fallen in love with another man and they are to marry. Whatever will he do? Karl Franz again decides he must fulfill his duty, marry Margaret, and serve out his days as King. He stoically trudges toward his exit.

At this point, we reprise his passionate love song from Act One, "Deep in My Heart, Dear." I must now attend to my music, but out of the corner of my eye I have seen the King turn, rush back to his beloved Kathie, and take her into his arms. As I play, he sings,

I've waited a lifetime for someone to say
The things you are saying to me,
And darling, believe every word that I say
Just look in my eyes and you'll see.
Your smile and my tears have all melted away
My worries were all false and naught.
It looks like the start of a beautiful day
Just holding you here in my arms.
With you every day's a beautiful day
As long as I'm here in your arms.

The show ends. I don't know all of the details, but it's clear to me from the music that the King and Kathie wind up together somehow in the classic ending, boy-gets-girl. I loved the show for its great tunes and romantic ending.

Flash forward eleven years. My fellow professor at The College of St. Rose, Mary Ann Craig, programmed the "Serenade" from *The Student Prince* on her faculty euphonium recital. Since there is a lovely duet version, she invited me to play the second part. As she introduced the piece, she summarized the story of the operetta, ending with how the King pledged his undying love to Kathie at the end, but then returned to Karlsberg to marry Princess Margaret.

Say *what?* But...how...why? The "Serenade" began, but my thoughts were on the tragedy of Karl Franz and Kathie's separation. I've rarely performed with my heart so filled with sorrow.

Speak Now or Forever Hold Your Piece

No, spelling Nazi, the title is NOT a typo. This section is about "Mute clams" and how they leave you holding your piece (instrument) in shock as the music passes by. If this word play bothers you, I sincerely apologize. Please imagine me comforting you with a hug while I pat you on the back and say, "There, their, they're."

Their *(sic)* are two big challenges for brass players at the opera. Well, three, if you listen to those wackos who think we play too loud. OK, four, if you include staying awake during Baroque *recitatives*—extended passages of sung dialogue with minimal (i.e. boring) accompaniment.

Sidebar: Think I'm kidding about those recitatives? My dentist uses them for a sedative, but the monotony has been known to drive some patients over the edge. I remember the time a dental assistant escorted me to the chair in the inner chamber, and I heard a patient scream, "No, no, no, I can't take one more rolled chord from the harpsichord! Please make it stop! I'd rather hear the drill and screaming children than another note of recitative!" (OK, I might have made some of that up, but we both know it could have happened.)

The first challenge an operatic brass player faces is to nail the challenging passage or random high note that can cause coronary and digestive problems from the stress leading up to it. (See *Neurotic clam.*) Fortunately, we have all spent years practicing those very excerpts, and we probably even played them for the audition that landed us the job. But an even bigger, though seemingly mundane challenge is to make sure that the first note speaks after sitting through a prolonged tacet section.

Allen Ostrander, bass trombonist with the NBC Symphony and New York Philharmonic, told me about one of his earliest experiences playing for Toscanini. The piece was *An American in Paris*. When the time came for the rubato seven-note bass trombone solo, Allen had his horn in place, watched for his cue, and started to play. But the first note did not speak! He froze, knowing the maestro's infamous temper. Then Toscanini's glare seemed to will the music right out of him. He played the solo merely a second late and all went well from there.

The bass trombone part in Mozart's *Don Giovanni* contains what I contend is the most difficult note in the repertoire. The trombones don't even play for the first two-and-a-half hours of the opera. When we first enter, the bass trombone is supposed to play a low D, very softly. Or if you have a sadistic maestro, very *very* softly. And the rest of the orchestra tries to play even more softly than you, because the strings secretly hate the low brass section and like to see us suffer. I've seen their smirks, sitting with those books full of music in front of them, knowing that composers love them the best. True, it has only been twenty minutes since you got to warm up during the last intermission, but your lips and horn have cooled down and you're still burping up that cheap cola you had to help you stay awake. And now the bassoonist in front of you has moved and you have to lean over sideways to see the downbeat. If you don't get the note to speak softly, in tempo, in tune, and with a good tone, it will no doubt sound like a cow fart.

So as the appointed time of execution draws near, if you sneak a look into the back row of the pit you will see me blowing warm air through my horn, moving my left hand from spot to spot on the bell to warm it evenly, emptying the water that condensed in my slide so the sound doesn't gurgle (dear God, please don't let me forget this step!), and massaging my lips as if trying to bring them back from the dead. Oh, that Mozart. Ya gotta love his sense of humor.

Bass Trombone Part for *Madame Butterfly*

In the first line of music you see five notes, followed by a long tacet section. The next two lines show a few cues that will, hopefully, awaken you in time to play the short, loud B-flat—ideally without creating an unexpected solo if you miscount. Two more notes are played, then you can get back to reading or snoozing through the next tacet. You must decipher two more cues and a hodgepodge of rests in order to join in on the D-flat that pops up in the middle of nowhere. After another tacet, the first trombone plays in the fifth measure of 47, scaring the bejeebers out of you as you think you missed your entrance. Just another day in the life...

Phantom of the Stanley

At various times I brought one or more of my sons along to a rehearsal at the Stanley Theater in Utica, N.Y. They loved to sit up in the balcony and explore the secret passage that runs under the length of the large vaudeville era theater. Beneath the backstage area, several dark dank rooms surround the tunnel entrance. The dimly lit walls are lined with autographed posters of various headliners from the past, while water gurgles eerily in the tunnel's drainage culvert. I was happy to learn that in spite of the recent major renovations the Stanley has enjoyed, the bowels of the Theater still retain the secret passage and Phantom of the Opera atmosphere.

Pits like the one at the Stanley have an elevator lift beneath them in order to adjust the height of the musicians' platform. The pit begins at ground level for egress, and then when all the doors have been secured, someone backstage flips the switch to raise the pit to the desired level. Without fail, as soon as the doors are closed someone will call out, "Beam me up, Scotty!" or "Energize!"

The Pit of Glimmerglass

The Glimmerglass pit is superior to many, though it does have its pitfalls. (Sorry.) Chief among these is the back row. The main part of the pit consists of a large platform about two feet higher than the back row, where the ceiling slopes downward. This forms a trough between the rear wall and the rest of the pit. Of course, this is where the trombone section most often sits. Imbedded in the ceiling are nozzles for the emergency sprinkler system, strategically placed to be certain one is always directly above my seat. The ceiling is already so low that when I stand for the bows I must remember to duck my head. Ducking the sprinklers is just a bonus.

There is barely enough room in the back row to fit a chair and to wedge a music stand up against the main platform, where the favored members of the orchestra get to sit. Guess which instrument would have the most difficulty playing in that space? If you guessed the one whose primary moving part requires extending the forward reach of the instrument by a couple of feet, you are indeed correct. Fortunately, I must lean back a bit in order to see the conductor on his penthouse podium, so this allows my trombone slide to clear the edge of the platform—where it is free to rendezvous with a chair leg or instrument case in the bassoon section. Except for the production of *Salome*, when the French horn section sat directly in front of us. (*Salome* is the story of the beheading of John the Baptist, complete with his head on a serving tray.) This put the expanded horn section's bells directly at face level, not unlike facing a firing squad—if the squad is made up of musical cannons—and since my ears are attached to the sides of my face, they were treated to the horn section's full range of dynamic nuance. *Nuance?* It's freakin' Strauss, they were merciless.

So if you were in the audience for that production and enjoyed the magnificent horn section, you've got nothing on me. I got to enjoy it *twice*: first, upon blastoff as the sound shot past my ears, and again when it ricocheted off the back wall on its way out to you, our beloved patrons. Ear plugs were supplied, but whenever I wore them it sounded to me as if I were playing into a mound of wet cotton, so I gave up and went *au naturel*. As I staggered out to the parking lot each night, my brain felt like it was vibrating. How did I recover from this onslaught? I got into my car and fired up a recording of *Chicago's* "If It Were You" at a volume that would make a metalhead wince. Something about that opening guitar slide, the driving bass line, and the screaming brass licks helped relieve the Straussian angst. By the time I reached U.S. 20, the song had purged my system enough to switch to a nice ballad or four: perfect for the white-knuckle drive through the fog bank north of Cherry Valley.

When not condemned to the "trough," the trombone section is most often situated on the left side of the pit, where the only time we need to duck is if something flies off the stage. It is my favorite place to play because it affords the best view of the rest of the orchestra. Since I usually have more rests than notes, it gives a good vantage point from which to watch and learn as my very gifted colleagues play. No matter where the trombones sit, we are among the first to arrive at the bathroom or coffee machine during intermission, and we are always the first to get to the parking lot after the show.

Meet the Glimmerglass Orchestra

Opera stars come and opera stars go. The singers in the Young Artists Program and chorus come and go. Artistic directors, general managers, production staff, and administrative staff are here one season, many of them are gone the next. The one element of any opera company that can truly be called its heart and soul is its orchestra. This is particularly true at Glimmerglass. As we enter our 40th season, I especially want to mention the orchestra members who have played in the pit since the very beginning: Michael Cleveland (violin), Janet Nepke (cello), and Ben Aldridge (trumpet).

It's not easy to play an accent on the flute or piccolo, but Floyd Hebert and Linda Greene manage to add such delightful nuance to their lines. Maybe their body language helps? Eileen

Whalen's heavenly oboe sound is like another voice in the opera, often expressing emotions too deep for words; like Robin Seletsky's clarinet solo in *Tosca* or her outstanding Klezmer[27] playing. Spencer "Fred" Phillips is tall and slender; when he plays his bassoon, it is almost as if he and the instrument are a single being. Nancy Dimock (Oboe 2), Tom Slavisky (Clarinet 2), and Mark Timerman (Bassoon 2) play the perfect "second fiddles" to the first chairs: matching tones and pitches through difficult woodwind passages is a bit like Ginger Rogers matching Fred Astaire step for step, only backwards.

Before her retirement, I was blessed to hear principal hornist Julia Hasbrouck Clay for more than thirty years, both at Glimmerglass and in the various orchestras in the region. If someone says they heard her crack a note once, don't believe it, it's an urban legend. Julia's legacy lives on through her students, her friends, and the beautiful artwork she now paints, proving there *is* life after the pits.

Historical sidebar. The French horn section is the only one with four distinct parts. This dates back to the days when horns had no valves and were best utilized to play the notes in the overtone series in which they were pitched. For example, the composer might write for a pair of horns pitched in D and a pair in A. Thus, horn players each carried a case with slides that could be changed to put the horn in a different key. With the development of valves in the first half of the 19th century, horns were able to enjoy chromatic playing and no longer needed the case of extra slides. Thanks to the Master Affiliation of French horn Instrumentalists Association (M.A.F.I.A.), composers have to this day been required to write four distinct horn parts. The musicians union did gain one concession: the horn players must keep one hand in the bell at all times.

Sociological sidebar: Over the years, I have observed that each of the four parts attracts a certain personality type. Principal horn players are the superheroes of the brass section. Their dramatic melodic lines must soar above the fray like Superman on a mission. Their lips must have the ability to pick out high notes with the utmost precision, since any note will sound with any valve combination when you're playing that high. (I am not making this up.) Unlike the principal trumpet, the lead horn must often play *softly* in the high register. This is like asking an aerialist to perform without a net. There is no room for self doubt if you want to sit in the principal horn chair, you must be invincible. One missed note will cause heads to turn. Two missed notes will cause *your* head to roll. Traditionally, the second horn part usually plays lower notes than

---

[27] A traditionally itinerant Jewish folk music of eastern Europe performed in a small band, as at weddings.

the third part, since it was the lower of the first pair of valveless horns. Today, this causes a situation in which second horn players think they are the second best players in the section, but the third chair players *know* they are second best because their parts are higher—besides, they sometimes get the melodies the composer withheld from the principal horns to keep them humble. The fourth horn player is either a converted trumpet player, a wannabe tuba player, or a former principal hornist who has fallen victim to kryptonite.

As for the Glimmerglass horns, Gabe Kovach is our reigning superhero. Patti O'Connell is the high school band director in Vestal, N.Y and plays horn in various opera, orchestra, and chamber music groups in the southern tier of the state. Aaron Brask, fourth horn, plays in the Jacksonville Symphony in Florida, he has filled in as principal horn at Glimmerglass, and he has a couple of recordings available, which can be found at his website: www.lasthorn.com.

The upper floor of the dressing rooms are supported by a series of posts. During intermission, we often found hornist Marty Burke leaning against the first post, which now has a brass nameplate designating it the official Martin Burke Leaning Post.

We lost our beloved tuba player, Chuck England, in January of 2009. I knew he wasn't feeling well during the 2008 season, but I was shocked to hear that a month later his health had taken a critical turn. Chuck was a giant of a man, both in stature and in spirit. I've heard most of the world's finest tuba players of our generation, and no one had a tone that surpassed Chuck's. I learned a lot about musicianship playing next to him for more than thirty years. His sound was so rich in overtones it was nearly impossible to play out of tune—though I did manage to find a way, now and again.

Wondering how we'd ever replace Chuck at Glimmerglass, I headed off to hear the auditions in New York City with a heavy heart. The audition facility was a basement room, complete with pipes and ducts running along the low ceiling—a serviceable replica of many pit conditions. (Honestly, though, ours is a fine pit in which to play, as long as you aren't a trombone player in the trough.) I am delighted to report that we were blessed to hear—and hire—David Saltzman as our new principal tuba. Not only did he play extremely well, he was the only one who produced a sound that came close to Chuck's. We found out after the audition that he had studied for a summer with Chuck at Hartwick College.

At that same set of auditions we heard applicants for the principal trumpet and trombone positions. Recently retired, Carleton Clay (trumpet) and Don Robertson (trombone) had been founding members of the Glimmerglass Orchestra.

Carleton has served as principal trumpet in most of the orchestras and chamber groups of Central New York, and he has had a distinguished career as a composer, university professor, and impresario. He has hired me for many gigs over the years. Don still teaches at SUNY Binghamton and plays trombone in various groups, following a stellar teaching career in Bainbridge, N.Y.

For those three brass openings we had 364 applicants in 2010. We were unable to extend audition invitations to several people with doctoral degrees in performance from major institutions because their resumés were not as strong as those we invited. We were confident we had a good pool of players to choose from.

The first trumpet player out of the box that Monday morning, Jerry Bryant, nailed the excerpts and played a wonderful solo. He had stiff competition but secured the job by knocking every pitch we threw him out of the park. Jerry is our current principal trumpet and personnel manager.

One trombone applicant in particular delivered a superb rendition of the high solo from Ravel's "Bolero." He made the final round so, of course, we asked him to play it again. Another perfect performance. Greg Spiridopoulos was our clear winner.

While chosen for their vituoso playing, David, Jerry, and Greg are all great additions to the orchestra personality-wise.

Ben Aldridge (trumpet 2) had played alongside Carleton Clay for decades. Back in the 1980s I took some students to hear the two of them perform the Vivaldi "Concerto for Two Trumpets," and a couple of kids complained afterward that they couldn't tell who was playing what part because they sounded so much alike. High praise, indeed. Ben is a staunch New York Yankees fan, but we forgive him.

Danny Martin, second trombone, is hands-down the best jazzer in the orchestra. He recently retired from a terrific career as band director in Laurens, N.Y, a small school district whose marching, concert, and jazz bands routinely won annual competitions against much larger school districts. As I mentioned elsewhere, he has earned special recognition for his willingness to nudge me if I was in danger of missing an entrance while entranced with reading or writing during a long tacet.

Our harpist, André Tarantiles, has performed as a soloist and accompanist with an impressive list of headliners, shows, and concert halls, and he is the official harpist at St. Patrick's Cathedral in N.Y. City. André's worst gig was the time he played with *ABBA* at a dance club called "Sam Frank's." He's no disco fan, but the pay was too good to pass up. By the end of the night, he was in such a hurry to leave that it wasn't until he pulled into his driveway that he realized, "I left my harp in Sam Frank's disco!"

Joe Mone, percussionist, retired a few years back. I had the chance to play a few gigs over the years with his Big Band, and every year the Glimmerglass pit looked forward to the night he treated us to platters of shrimp. That was when I started carrying a toothbrush in my case. Believe me, you don't want to sit in the middle of a brass section after someone has had seafood, onions, garlic, a lot of booze, too much beans or broccoli. Yeah, maybe a lot of people wouldn't want to sit in the middle of a brass section under any conditions, but the rest of the orchestra has survived this long, so don't believe the horror stories you hear from those who sit near us.

Our tympanist, Kathy Lowery, has been a member of the orchestra for over 25 years and has also logged tens of thousands of miles on U.S. 20 in order to play at Glimmerglass. Jeff Grubbs plays principal percussion in several upstate New York groups. Our new principal percussionist, Matthew McClung, spent two months studying drumming techniques in Ghana. It is probably not true that he was hired in hopes that his experience in Africa might come in handy when fending off the prehistoric insects that sometimes emerge in the pit, but I did see him execute an impressive triple ratamacue[28] on a ten-inch millipede last summer.

Which brings us to the string section. There are so *many* of them, where do I start? I have to admit, I've rarely had an extended conversation with most of them. It isn't like we never have the opportunity, but in large music ensembles it seems as if the musicians tend to hang out with members of their own "species"— although our former oboist, Vicki Rickard, played trombone in her college jazz band and seemed to feel at home with the beings on the "dark side" of the orchestra. There are other exceptions, as explained in the following sidebar.

Sociological sidebar: Some bass players fit in comfortably with the brass because they double on tuba when the opportunity arises. Many can also lay down a hot rock or cool jazz line, if given the chance. Some cellists have a recessive brass player gene, as demonstrated by their willingness to wrestle with such an ungainly instrument for a living. If you ever see a female string player smoking a cigar, she is most likely a cellist. Violists are a breed apart, the key word being "apart." They are the butt of many jokes that imply—oh alright, come right out and state—that they are inferior to violinists. But if you want to open a Pandora's box, get a violist a little tipsy and brace yourself for the stories you will hear. The violins are divided into two sections: those who *know* they are the most important part of the orchestra, and those who aspire to be the best but prefer to dodge the pressure by playing second fiddle. Sitting on the inside of the orchestra and away from the audience's view allows the second

---

[28] A triple ratamacue is a complex snare drum rhythm with twenty-four taps. For a video, go to: www.youtube.com/watch?v=OOrttvxjOrw

violins to save money by buying their concert attire at K-Mart. If their parents chide them about playing second violin for a career, they can always point out that at least they aren't violists.

So as for the Glimmerglass violins, Concertmaster Ruotao Mao was born in Beijing, graduated from New England Conservatory, and has a long list of awards and international performing experiences to his credit. Liz Silver was my son's violin teacher before he began euphonium, then it was goodbye to the violin. Ann-Marie Schwartz competes in ballroom dancing. It must have been fate: George Myers secretly gave a stuffed toy cow to Jennifer Reuning, and then hit a cow on his way back from a Glimmerglass rehearsal. So, of course, they got married. Michael Cleveland has been a tireless contract negotiator for us for years. Nick Ross earned a doctoral degree in conducting and has had some wonderful orchestral conducting experiences (I'm so jealous.) Kathe Hannauer is a fellow Ithaca grad who lives in N.Y. City and plays in the Broadway pits. Faina Agranov grew up in Eastern Europe and won many prizes as a soloist and chamber player in Russia and Europe before establishing her career in the U.S. During the academic year, Heather Wittels plays violin with Chicago Lyric Opera. Raymond Zoeckler has been playing violin all over upstate New York for decades. Sasha Margolis appeared as a strolling violinist in the hit TV series "Lost." Leona Nadj still returns to her native Croatia to perform and has played in the pit of several top Broadway shows. Sue Rabut hails from Boston and is an outstanding Baroque violinist. Xiaoqing Yu was born in China and now teaches at Lee University in Tennessee. Victoria Stewart spent two years in Seoul on a Fulbright Scholarship. Ubaldo Valli is a fellow Ithaca grad who heads up the annual Pierstown Concert Series: programs of chamber music performed by members of the Glimmerglass Orchestra.

Our previous concertmaster of 22 years, Michael Levin, played with the Metropolitan Opera. He was an avid swimmer who enjoyed taking the two-mile swim across Lake Otsego after one of those hot and humid matinees. We lost him due to complications following surgery in 2009.

Among the viola section, Christine Ims keeps an active performance schedule in the New York metropolitan area. Katrina Smith used a Fulbright grant to study Baroque violin in The Hague. Megan Dyer teaches in the Oneonta school district and was formerly principal violist with Tri-Cities Opera. Dee Dee Fancher is a fellow dog lover and plays with the Columbus Symphony. Christine Orio loves to perform bluegrass, country, and Irish fiddling. Alexandra Van de Geijn performs in a variety of venues in the Baltimore-D.C. area.

Principal cellist Janet Nepke, a founding member of the orchestra, has enjoyed an active career in performance, teaching, and the business of music, particularly the issue of copyright law. Ruth Berry earned her graduate degree in Musicology from Cornell, plays Baroque cello, and performs and teaches in Georgia. Susan Libby performs with the Albany Symphony; we both played in the 1985 performance of "Scheherezade" in which Leo Mahigian, in his first concert back following the death of his wife, delivered the most heartfelt violin solos I have heard. Ben Whittenburg performs with many regional orchestras in the Northeast and in the Broadway pits.

Jon Pascolini is Assistant Principal Bass with the Dayton Philharmonic and Principal with the West Virginia Symphony. Dave Irvin teaches at Delaware Academy in Delhi, N.Y. and plays bass in several regional orchestras.

Our theorboist, Michael Leopold, travels the world as both a soloist and an accompanist. He earned his degree in lute and theorbo from L'Istituto di Musica Antica della Accademia Internazionale della Musica[29] in Milan, Italy.

Just as the orchestra is the heart and soul of the opera, the string section is the orchestra's atrium and ventricles. Or maybe the aorta and vena cava? Well, you know what I mean. A good example is one of my all-time favorite moments in music, the heartbreakingly beautiful "Intermezzo" in Pietro Mascagni's *Cavalleria Rusticana*.[30] If you don't know this piece, take the time to log on to YouTube and have a listen. http://www.youtube.com/watch?v=7OvsVSWB4TI

Go ahead, do it now. I'll wait for you.

Highest Paid Player (per note)

The standard contract provides for a pay scale built around a set wage per service, be it a rehearsal or performance. Additional fees are based on working overtime, for serving as principal in the section, and for doubling on additional instruments. The amount of time one plays during the service is not a factor. It is quite common for the brass and percussion to be excused when the rest of the rehearsal does not include them.

To celebrate the opening of the new Glimmerglass opera house in 1987, William Schuman composed *Cooperstown Fanfare* for two trumpets and two trombones. We played the fanfare from the

---

[29] This is also an excellent school to attend if you like cheerleading, since they need 63 cheerleaders to spell out the school name. The sports teams aren't very good, though. The school name on the team jerseys makes them hang down below the players' knees.

[30] Even worse than the impending tragedy on stage, the trombones do not play at all in the "Intermezzo."

front balcony at every performance, fifteen and five minutes before the curtain. The company paid us extra for playing this since it was counted as overtime, unless we did not play in the opera that followed, in which case we were paid the full service fee—for a total of two minutes worth of playing. On those days we were often in our cars heading out of the parking lot as the rest of our colleagues played the opera overture. One downside to this situation was that none of us liked the fanfare. At all. After several years, the opera company switched to a fanfare arranged from the music in one of that season's operas. After several more years, the company eliminated the fanfares as a budget-saving measure.

At the opera, a glance at the thickness of the players' music books will clearly indicate who the workhorses are. In the case of the bass trombone part, the word "book" is a misnomer. Leaflet or pamphlet is often apropos, as in Monteverdi's Baroque opera *L'Orfeo*. The good news: it used five trombones. The bad news: my part consisted of only 176 notes on two pages, which is even worse than what I have to look forward to this summer of 2014, our third production of Puccini's *Madama Butterfly*, in which the bass trombone has 242 notes. Sixty of them occur in the last twenty bars of the three hour and fifteen minute opera. Yep, I'll get a lot of writing done this summer.

The best per note fee I've ever made was back in the 1980s, when the Catskill Symphony and René Prins performed Sibelius' lovely English horn solo, *The Swan of Tuonela*. It was the only piece on the program that employed the trombones. Our parts each consisted of one twelve-measure note, in my case, a low A. Oh, if only I could always command a fee of $90 per note. Let's see...that *Madama Butterfly* fee would be $21,780 per service—almost what an average major league baseball player makes per game.

Everybody's a Critic!

Critics: a necessary evil—or evil necessarily? As you can tell by now, I'm certainly willing to own up to my failures, but come on now, do critics really need to pile on?

The Albany *Times Union* sent a food critic to review the recent opening night of *Young Frankenstein* at Schenectady Light Opera, and while the show itself got a well-deserved rave, the pit orchestra was described as "...at best, barely competent." At least this reviewer wasn't as harsh as a *New York Times* critic who once characterized my colleague's tone as "a singularly ugly metallic whine." I'll bet critics sit around thinking up insults that they hope will make them sound clever.

My first reaction was, "Hey, I've played far worse than that."

At that particular performance, while playing a French horn part on the bass trombone, I continued my dysfunctional relationship with high notes by producing a juicy Acrophobic Clam on a high A.

I do *not* want to wind up like that poor trumpeter, Ugo Solari, who at the age of 43 met his untimely demise whilst performing the closing notes of "The Impossible Dream" at the Il Torquo Jazz Club. He blew so hard while trying to hit a high note that "his head swelled and burst like a balloon," according to Pat Craigers in *The National Enquirer*. Patrons were splattered with blood. (It was printed in a newspaper, it must be true.)

The wonderful cast of *Young Frankenstein* had our backs, as evidenced by the note they sent us the next night:

"*We've all seen shows where the music is canned*
There's never the magic you get with a band!
We love the nuance and balance you bring
It gives us all a lift when we sing!
When we need a vamp, you're always there,
We want you to know, we notice, we care!
We're grateful for all the hard work that you do—
In other words—suck it T.U.!" *(Times Union)*

We dubbed ourselves "The Barely Competent Players." Our music director, Adrienne Sherman, bought us each a coffee mug or flask with our new name. What else could we do but make sure the rest of the run was the best we could play?

Top Ten Reasons the Trumpet is the Best Instrument

10. Trumpets play the melody more often than any other brass instrument.

9. Trumpet players only use three fingers to operate the instrument; French horns, euphoniums, and tubas use four or more. This leaves two fingers free for other activities.[31]

8. NASA chose Louis Armstrong to be the first man to walk on the moon.

7. The trumpet is the only orchestral instrument you can play with one hand, leaving the other hand free to hold your drink; or better yet, play two trumpets at once.[32]

6. The trumpet is the only instrument that gets to play Reveille. (Oh... 5:00 AM. Never mind.)

5. Does your sports team need encouragement? There's a good reason they don't call a violinist to play "Charge!"

4. Whether you're talking about trumpets or strumpets, you get what you pay for.

3. The business end of the trumpet is at ear level of the musician seated in front of you. That extortion money comes in handy.

2. Assembling the instrument couldn't be easier: you just stick the buzzer thingy into the end of the horn with the smallest hole.

1. The Bible says God will raise the dead with the sound of a trumpet. We audition for this job every time we pick up our horns.

---

[31] Nose-picking is not recommended unless you have very long fingers—or a very big nose.

[32] This is a *must see* video of one person playing two trumpets. https://www.youtube.com/watch?v=KV9b7Vuvaw8

Trombones! Trombones!

During the final bows at nearly every opera performance, several people in the audience call out, "Bravo! Bravo!" Back in the 1990s one gentleman yelled "BravO! BravO!" and we in the back row thought it sounded like, "TrombOnes! TrombOnes!" Since then, it is not uncommon for one of us in the trombone section to call out, "TrombOnes! TrombOnes!" Oddly, no one else in the orchestra seems to be as amused by this as we are.

I don't recall the production, but several years back I went to Glimmerglass on one of my days off to see an opera that included only two trombones. At the end I proudly lauded my colleagues with, "TrombOnes! TrombOnes!" I can't believe I was the only one.

The trombone section did receive its own solo bow in one performance, when Jirka Kratochvil led the Catskill Choral Society in a Czech arrangement of Mozart's magnificent *Requiem*. The trombones doubled nearly all of the vocal lines, resulting in one of my all-time favorite choral concert experiences. Bonus: maestro Kratochvil proved to be an outstanding orchestral conductor, as well.

If You're Going to Take Photos of Young Women at a Motel, You Better Invite a Chaperone

Honestly, this story does wind up involving my experiences as a pit musician, stay with me...

While preparing my Civil War novel, *The Unfinished Work*, for initial publication in 2007 by Trafford Books, we had originally decided to search for Civil War era photographs that might represent the lead character's two love interests, 17-year-old Eliza and her 15-year-old sister, Kathleen, and then to incorporate those photos into the design for the back cover of the book. Serendipity intervened.

During that time I was invited to photograph a local production of *Fiddler on the Roof*. In the midst of shooting hundreds of photos, a young woman turned around and there before me stood the face I had imagined as Kathleen! How could I not want to use her picture on the book? I then recognized her as Ann Henry, one of my son's high school choir students. Realizing the inappropriateness of approaching her with the idea, I sought out her mother and quickly explained what I had in mind. She asked what the book was about. When I told her that it was a Civil War novel about the Battle of Hanover based heavily on fact, and that the character of Kathleen was a fictional cousin to a real-life character named Lydia Wertz, she stopped me. "Oh, we have relatives in Hanover named Wertz." You guessed it. Ann Henry is related to the real-life cousin of the character I had imagined her portraying. I still get a chill every time I recount this story. I was delighted she agreed to be part of the project.

But now I needed to find someone to portray Eliza. On my way into the pit for the next performance at Glimmerglass, I walked past one of the orchestra interns, Jamie Leigh Sampson, who on this day wore her hair up and was not wearing her glasses. Could she be Eliza? I don't recall having ever spoken with her outside of the usual pleasantries between coworkers. During the first act, I snuck glances at her as she sat at the far end of the pit next to her fellow intern and fiancé, Andrew. Yes, she could be Eliza.

I hurried outside during the intermission, told her about the project, and asked her if she would like to take part. Her reaction surprised me. Relief?

Jamie explained that she had noticed me looking at her during the first act. Of course, I had been very careful to avoid making eye contact, so how had she known? (*Mysteries of Life #12*: Women *always* know when they are being observed.) She had already alerted Andrew, "We might have a problem with Frank," so she was much relieved to learn my intentions were honorable. Her enthusiasm for the project was so great, I gave her photocopies of hairstyles and dresses from the May 1863 issue of *Godey's Lady's*

Book, and she made a dress and styled her hair authentically. She and Andrew even planned a future vacation around coming to Gettysburg to visit with me while I signed copies of the book at the 145th Anniversary reenactment of the battle in 2008.

Next, we had to decide where to shoot the photos. Jamie suggested we take them a couple of miles down the road, at the residence building where she lived with many of the opera staff. I quickly agreed and we arranged a time. Then it hit me. That residence building used to be the Deer Run Motel. Jamie lived in a former motel room. Had I just arranged to take pictures of two beautiful young women at a motel? That sounded more than a little sordid. Now what?

I decided to invite my wife and Ann's mother and brother to come along, and then we all went out to dinner. Problem solved.

Jamie and Andrew later asked me to be their wedding photographer. They went on to grad school for music composition, I commissioned Jamie to compose a piece for our brass quintet, and she is enjoying much success in her music career. Ann went on to attend my alma mater, Ithaca College, and she recently finished grad school in Boston.

Jamie Leigh Sampson and Ann Henry

Close Calls

We've probably all said at one time or another, "The show must go on." But that is not necessarily true. Here are a few of my close calls.

In March of 2000, the *Hartwick Trombone Quartet* was invited to perform Jan Koetsier's *Concertino* with the U.S. Army Orchestra at the Eastern Trombone Workshop in Fort Myer, VA. Just before the afternoon rehearsal I came down with a debilitating migraine headache. The other trombonists—Hal Reynolds, Don Robertson, and Dan Martin—had to scramble to find someone to fill in for me, just in case I couldn't recover in time. One of the Army Band members rehearsed the piece with them. Fortunately for me, I was well enough to play the performance that night. Unfortunately for my three colleagues, their chops had to work overtime due to the extra rehearsal with the sub. The performance was well received, and we were invited back to play the piece the following year in its arrangement with band accompaniment. By that time, Hartwick College had withdrawn its funding for the group, so we changed our name to the *Glimmerglass Trombone Quartet.* A third arrangement of the *Concertino* exists with piano accompaniment. Perhaps the Workshop will invite us to play it if we change our name a third time?

Since the Glimmerglass Festival is a summer venue, we are subject to the effects of nature, such as hot and humid matinees, the pungent aroma of manure spread on a nearby field, or a major thunderstorm. Several times a thunderclap or lightning bolt timed out perfectly with a dramatic moment on stage. Sometimes we have lost power for an extended period of time, like during the 1987 season when maestro Stewart Robertson played piano in the pit while the opera continued on a stage lit only by the emergency lights.

A few years earlier, I had conducted the Guilderland Town Band in a series of outdoor concerts. On one memorable night, guest artist Dave Unland had just begun his tuba solo, Don Haddad's *Suite for Tuba and Band,* when a lightning bolt crackled nearby. The image of the next day's newspaper headline flashed in my mind: "Tuba Player Struck by Lightning." I cut Dave's cadenza short and we finished the piece just as the storm came upon us. The audience fled for cover. Since the rest of the band was well protected under the roof of the band shell, I decided to go ahead with the final piece, a medley from *Star Wars*. We couldn't have asked for better special effects than the booming thunder and laser-like lightning bolts.

A circuit tripped in the pit during the 2013 season at Glimmerglass, leaving most of the woodwind section without light. Since I was in the midst of a tacet section, I turned on my iPhone's Flashlight App and held the phone over the bassoons' music so they could play until light was restored. The only notes I missed were doubled in the bassoon, anyway.

Later that season I lifted my trombone to play, but it snagged on something on the way to my mouth. My shoelace had lassoed the spit valve lever! I tugged, thinking the lace would untie and free the horn. It did not. The moment to play was almost upon me. I wiggled the horn and my leg, attempting to work the horn free. Just when it looked like I would have to play while moving my leg in sync with the slide, the lace finally worked free. Of course, that wouldn't have happened if we were allowed to play barefoot. On the other hand, there are those puddles in front of the brass players' chairs...

How Did the Well Go Dry?

During the 1970s and 1980s my brass quintet performed a few dozen concerts each year, mostly in schools, that were funded by the Music Performance Trust Fund. This fund was established in 1948 via an agreement between the musicians' union and the recording industry. A royalty from each recording sold went into this fund in order to pay for free, public concerts performed by union musicians. When I was first involved, we had to have a sponsor contribute a nominal donation of $25 to the fund, then each musician was paid $25 and the "leader" received $50. So for our quintet, a $25 donation yielded $150 in payments. By the mid-1980s, the pay scale had risen to $40, but the sponsor had to contribute the same amount that the concert would cost, so our quintet concert cost the sponsor the same $240 that the fund would pay out. Huh?

I know there are fewer recordings sold these days, and I know the fund has overhead to pay, but where does all the money go that the recording industry provides each year if the sponsors are basically funding the concerts themselves? I can't help but wonder if the fund is run by the Master Affiliation of French horn Instrumentalists Association. Too bad, because we can no longer play those free school concerts, and I miss seeing the expressions of delight on the kids' faces.

Frank of La Mancha

The Broadway musical *Man of La Mancha* has played a significant part in my musical career. I grew up in the 1960s, when dozens of performers sang their renditions of Don Quixote's iconic song, "The Impossible Dream," which was all I knew of the show until we played a medley of the show's music in a high school band concert in 1970. I instantly fell in love with the mixed meters and lilting melodies, though all I knew of the story was that Don Quixote was the main character. My first experience as a conductor was directing The King's College Concert Band in the medley from *Man of La Mancha* during my sophomore year in college.

I've played in the pit for the show five times: two college productions, a community theater production, the 1997-98 national tour, and in the 2012 production for which I was the stage director. The '97-'98 tour starred Robert Goulet, hands down the best actor I've seen and heard in the role, including Brian Stokes Mitchell's superb performance in the Broadway revival, a second national tour, and two regional productions.

During the tour performances at Proctor's Theater in Schenectady, they divided the pit in half and seated us in the frontmost boxes on either side of the stage. We had monitors in order to hear each other; it worked, but it felt like I had to play along with a recording. At least I had a decent view of the stage and was able to study Mr. Goulet's performance night after night; he was a model of excellence and consistency. I wish you could have heard his gripping performance of the monologue where he, as Cervantes, speaks of his life experiences:

I have lived nearly fifty years, and I have seen life as it is. Pain, misery, hunger...cruelty beyond belief. I have heard the singing from taverns and the moans from bundles of filth on the streets. I have been a soldier and seen my comrades fall in battle...or die more slowly under the lash in Africa. I have held them in my arms at the final moment. These were men who saw life as it is, yet they died despairing. No glory, no gallant last words...only their eyes filled with confusion, whimpering the question, "Why?" I do not think they asked why they were dying, but why they had lived. When life itself seems lunatic, who knows where madness lies? Perhaps to be too practical is madness. To surrender dreams—this may be madness. To seek treasure where there is only trash. Too much sanity may be madness—and maddest of all: to see life as it is, and not as it should be!

Dale Wasserman, *Man of La Mancha*

Night after night, this was one of the most dramatic moments I've seen in any theater. Sadly, this monologue is usually breezed through without creating the corresponding mental images and plumbing the emotional depths of Cervantes' thoughts and memories.

Another of my favorite moments was the staging of "Little Bird, Little Bird," during which Mr. Goulet enters as Miguel de Cervantes teaching one of the muleteers the song. In this production, Michael Goulet, Robert's son, played the role of the muleteer. Not only was their duet marvelous, but the audience thoroughly enjoyed the father and son moment. But I can top that with two of my own father and son experiences with this show.

In 2001 I had the privilege to perform the lead role in a community theater production. My son, Nathan, played the role of Sancho Panza; my son, Jonathan, played the Innkeeper; my son, Christopher, played bass trombone; and my wife, Betsy, played clarinet. It was the only production we have all been in together.

In a wonderful bit of serendipity, the Aldonza to my Quixote was Susan Pendergast, who later became Jonathan's mother-in-law. Our kids grew up together sharing community theater and music, along with kids who have remained their closest friends in their adult lives. We never had to worry about the crowd they hung out with while growing up. I credit music and theater with playing major roles in shaping them into the amazing adults they have all become.

On a less fortunate note, perhaps, is the event that led to the "immortalization" of one area actor. Ian Devine, one of the muleteers, took advantage of his time offstage to "see a man about a horse." Unfortunately, his wireless mic was still live. The event was broadcast into the house—earning him the nickname, "Peein' Ian."

Three kind folks came up to me after the show and said they enjoyed my performance even more than that of Richard Kiley, the originator of the role on Broadway. To any degree that was so, I have to attribute it to my chance to study and emulate the great Robert Goulet.

My other father and son experience was in 2012, when I was the stage director for the show with the Not So Common Players in Clifton Park. N.Y. The run garnered seven TANYS awards, including one for my son, Jonathan, as the music director. He also played the roles of a muleteer and the Padre; more on that later.

Shawn Morgan, our Cervantes, delivered a stirring monologue, I'm happy to report, and our Aldonza, Elisa Verb, was among the very best in the role I have ever seen. Both of the leads won TANYS awards, and the entire cast was superb in every way.

I played in the pit and conducted, as necessary. During one scene, I even got the chance to include a trombone sound effect I had discovered in junior high. If the trombone slide is removed and put back on so that it is only connected to the tube attached to the mouthpiece, then you can produce a rather convincing "moo" effect as the sound comes out of the free end of the slide. I had our Aldonza "milk a cow" during the stable scene, and surprised her with the sound effect during the final dress rehearsal. It's always fun to try to make an actor break character—but only during a rehearsal. I played it in the performances, and thankfully no one on stage snickered.

One of my most remarkable theatrical experiences came during the rehearsals. Once, when Elisa was unable to attend, Heather-Liz Copps filled in for that run-through. Heather-Liz had originally wanted to audition for Aldonza, but I told her I was looking for an older actor for that part. When she accepted the role of Antonia (for which she earned a TANYS award), I asked her to cover the role of Aldonza, promising her the opportunity to play the part in a rehearsal, during which she could feel free to use the book and skip any of the songs, if she liked. When the night came, she delivered a marvelous performance—off book, hitting all the marks, and singing every note. As a director, it was quite a relief to know the show wouldn't suffer if something happened to our wonderful Elisa.

Unexpectedly, I even had the chance to cover the lead role in a run-through when Shawn was unavoidably detained. It was pretty ragged, I freely admit, but it is one of those dream roles, so it was a blast to slog my way through it, even with a singing voice that had already lost what little quality it once had.

Several times our pianist, Adrienne Sherman, an outstanding musician and constantly in-demand music director, had to bail me out by cueing the pit's entrance. I would get so caught up in the show that I'd miss the dialogue cue.

Back in my days as a church choir director, when I conducted oratorios I sat in the front row during the unconducted arias. Once I was so taken with an aria that I forgot I was supposed to conduct the next number. I looked around, waiting to hear the next piece before it dawned on me that it wouldn't happen until I got off my butt and waved my arms. I was only in my early 20s at the time—that doesn't bode well for my future mental state, does it?[33]

A cast member from the 2001 production, Myleah Misenhimer, choreographed the 2012 production. I particularly enjoyed the *pas de deux* she crafted for my staging of "To Each His Dulcinea." Rather than the usual staging in which the Padre stands and sings while we see Aldonza preparing for her liaison with Pedro and Quixote preparing for his vigil, I staged a scene in which a bashful young man approached a pretty girl and asked her to dance. He overcame his awkwardness and they shared a beautiful moment in dance. Our actors, Sarah Moran and Dan Heath, are a couple in real life. Dan had come along to the auditions requesting a nonsinging role, wanting to be an unobtrusive part of the show and share the experience with Sarah. Watching him take to his role as a muleteer and seeing their obvious affection for one another had given me the idea of the new staging. Seeing them dance together was one of my favorite memories from the production. Myleah crafted a scene in which two untrained dancers wonderfully express the joy of falling

---

[33] I've already told my family that if they have to take care of me after I lose my mind, please feel free to play practical jokes on me. I won't remember and they may as well have a good time.

in love. Bonus: my son, Jonathan, gave a beautiful rendition of "To Each His Dulcinea."

My parents-in-law, Bill and Carol Hurd, saw every one of the school musicals my sons were in over the years and always had a themed cake made to celebrate. It was finally my turn:

And the Award Goes to...

Back in 1963 Richard Rodney Bennett, brother of the famous composer, arranger, and Broadway orchestrator Robert Russell Bennett, composed an opera entitled *The Mines of Sulphur*.[34] It received several performances before falling out of sight in the early 1970s. Glimmerglass produced a revival in 2004 and recorded a live performance for a very nice CD released on the Chandos label, conducted by our Music Director, Stewart Robertson. We were nominated for a Grammy Award. We did not win. As enjoyable as the music was to perform, I have to admit I have not yet been able to listen to the entire recording. The music is just too dissonant for my taste when not hearing it in its theatrical context.

---

[34] http://en.wikipedia.org/wiki/The_Mines_of_Sulphur

In 1999 Glimmerglass premiered *Central Park*, a tryptich of one-act operas that take place in New York City's Central Park. The production was broadcast on PBS in January of 2000, for which we were nominated for an Emmy Award. We did not win.

While directing that 2012 production of *Man of La Mancha* I mentioned earlier, I founded the one–member "Sardonic Theater Organization of New York." I nominated every member of the cast and production staff for an individual STONY Award based on something humorous or ironic about their performance. We all won! (And we have the certificates to prove it.)

7:59 PM Dinner at an 8:00 PM Show
***Adrienne Sherman, Music Director for* Young Frankenstein**
Schenectady Light Opera, May 17, 2014

Musical Jokes

Q: What do you call a beautiful woman on the arm of a trombonist?
A: A tattoo.

Q: What do you do with a dead violist?
A: Move him back a stand.　(As told to me by violist John Mazarak.)

Q: What is the range of a tuba?
A: About 20 yards, if you have a good arm.

Q: What do you call a trio consisting of Emanuel Ax, piano;
     Doug Yeo, bass trombone; and Yo-Yo Ma, cello?
A: The Lizzie Borden Trio (Ax, Yeo, Ma.)

Q: Which is larger, the violin or the viola?
A: They are the same size; the violinist's head is larger.
A: They are the same size; the violist's head is smaller.

Q: How do you define a gentleman?
A: Someone who knows how to play the bagpipes but doesn't.

Q: How can you tell which children on a playground belong to a
    string player?
A: They are the ones who don't know how to swing.

Q: How can you tell which little boy on a playground belongs to a bad
    trombonist?
A: He doesn't have an ear and he can't work the slide.

Q: Why did the chicken cross the road?
A: To prove to the possum that it could be done.
    Yeah, that isn't a music joke, but it is probably the only one of
Hal Reynolds' jokes I dare put in print. Besides, everyone needs a
possum joke in their arsenal.

Q: What has six legs and six teeth?
A: A banjo trio.

Q: What is a sitzprobe[35]?
A: It is the rehearsal where the orchestra sits in the pit while the
    singers probe for their notes on stage.

    During the first rehearsal of an aria, the maestro stops the
music and instructs the orchestra, "Add two beats to the bar before
measure 17. In measure 19 add a flat to the B and a sharp to the C.
Put a fermata over the third beat of bar 22, and cut the last beat of
measure 27." The musicians hurriedly mark the changes. The
maestro lifts the baton to resume the rehearsal but is interrupted by
the soprano on stage, "Maestro, what about my part?" The maestro
replies, "Oh, you just go ahead and sing it the same way you did
before."

---

[35] A *sitzprobe* is a seated rehearsal, the first rehearsal with both the singers
and the orchestra. The focus is on coordinating the two groups.

Name Dropping

Having had a career centered in upstate New York, I've had fewer opportunities to make music with internationally renowned composers and performers than my colleagues in major cities. Nevertheless, here are a few tidbits about some composers you probably won't hear elsewhere.

During my sophomore year at The King's College (1972-73), the music majors received word that an anonymous pianist from New York City wished to play a private recital—private as in highly secret. We were invited to come hear the performance in the college chapel, but we were cautioned not to tell anyone about it. Apparently, this pianist was very famous and no longer performed in public. He was not introduced and I don't recall what pieces he played, but I remember thinking the guy performed very well for a man who appeared to be about seventy years old. I was later told the man's name: *Vladimir Horowitz*. I was a young brass player and his name meant nothing to me at the time. Now I wish I had known enough to smuggle my portable cassette recorder[36] into the recital.

Aaron Copland: Following a concert of Copland's music in Brooklyn in 1974, my music theory professor, Dean Arlton, took me backstage and introduced me to America's preeminent classical composer. As we shook hands, I tried to speak but was unable to utter a word. Mr. Copland smiled, continued to shake my hand, and asked me if I was a musician. I finally found my voice and told him how studying his *Symphony No. 3* and performing his *Fanfare for the Common Man* had inspired me to pursue a career in music.[37] We chatted about his use of the Fanfare in the fourth movement of the Symphony, and how he had used the woodwinds to first introduce the fanfare. All the while, my heart raced—I was talking music with *the* Aaron Copland! Emboldened to speak my mind, I asked, "Have you ever considered writing music for the euphonium?" Now you have to understand, at that point there were less than ten published solos that had been written specifically for the euphonium, and none of them by any composers of international significance. If I could somehow manage to encourage someone of Aaron Copland's status to compose a euphonium solo or use it in his orchestral work, it would be historic—at least for the euphonium community. He again smiled and told me he had already written for the euphonium. My heart leapt! Was I about to hear of some obscure, unpublished work featuring the euphonium that I might help bring to light? Nope. He proceeded to tell me about the euphonium parts in a few of his

---

[36] Cutting edge technology back then.

[37] Another strong influence was his book, *What to Listen for in Music*.

orchestral compositions that he had transcribed for concert band. I explained that I was familiar with those pieces and had already had the pleasure of playing two of them, but before I could make a pitch for a solo work—so naive I was but, hey, you never know—my time with the great master was over. Others had gathered to speak with him and I had to move along and give them a chance.

Leonard Bernstein: I met Mr. Bernstein the first time at a record-signing party in Manhattan in the mid-1970s. He kindly agreed to autograph one of his Mahler recordings for me, along with the scores for his *Mass* and his obscure brass ensemble piece, *Shivaree*. I knew he had used the melody from this brass piece in his much more famous *Mass*, so I asked him which piece he had written first. He frowned—or was it a glower?—and informed me that the *Shivaree* had been written first. He abruptly ended our conversation. It seemed to me as if he did not want anyone to know he had "borrowed" his own music, though plenty of other famous composers have done that throughout history. Several years later, I caught up with both Bernstein and Copland as they we getting into their limo after a performance at Tanglewood in Massachusetts. I had brought along my copies of the scores for Copland's *Symphony No. 3* and *Outdoor Overture*, hoping to get them autographed—and even daring to hope that one of them might recall our previous meeting. Mr. Copland smiled at me as I approached. I asked if he'd mind autographing the scores, but before he could reply, Mr. Bernstein waved me off, saying they had no time for autographs. Or was it because he remembered me from our previous encounter?

Alfred Reed: Mr. Reed was an internationally acclaimed composer of music for concert band, though he is virtually unknown in the orchestral world. At Ithaca College in 1978, I played euphonium in the premier of his outstanding five-movement suite for concert band, *Othello*, which features a couple of very romantic euphonium solo lines. During a Q&A session, someone asked Mr. Reed how he felt when he heard a bad performance of his music. He explained that it depended on the quality of the band playing the piece. It didn't bother him all that much if a "bad" band played his music poorly, because the audience would blame the band rather than the music. What bothered him was when a good band played his music poorly, because then the audience would think it was due to bad music, reflecting poorly on him as a composer. His words have guided me both as a performer and a conductor.

George Lloyd: I wrote earlier about the 1985 premier of his *Symphony No. 11*.[38] Mr. Lloyd, a neoromantic composer, also wrote pieces for Brass Band, which are very popular in his native England. The Brass Band sound inspired his orchestration of the new

---

[38] See page 41.

symphony, which is why he had included parts for the euphonium and the E-flat cornet. Thinking he would be receptive to the idea, I told him that if I could afford it, I would gladly commission him to write a concerto for euphonium and orchestra. He grinned and asked me how much money I thought I could get if I mortgaged my house. That was the moment when I discovered the limit to my love for the euphonium.

William Schuman: I met Mr. Schuman in 1987 during the gala opening of Glimmerglass' new opera house. His *New England Triptych,* one of my all-time favorite pieces of classical music, was originally written for orchestra, but he had also produced a concert band edition that features a hauntingly beautiful euphonium and cornet[39] duet at the beginning of the middle movement, "When Jesus Wept." By now I knew better than to ask him to write a piece of music unless I had at least $50,000 to offer for a commission fee. So I told him how much I enjoyed playing the euphonium in "When Jesus Wept" and that I admired his rewriting of the *Triptych* for concert band. He told me I could thank William Revelli[40] for that. Though Schuman had transcribed "When Jesus Wept" and "Chester" in the mid-1950s, "Be Glad Then, America" was not completed until 1975, primarily due to Dr. Revelli's continued requests. I asked Mr. Schuman if he had any new works in progress, hoping to create an opening to lobby for the euphonium. He said he had a few things in mind, but didn't mention anything in particular. I later learned that the next year he published *Chester Variations for Piano.* I'd like to think our conversation may have given him the idea to revisit that tune. Be that as it may, I've checked, and I'm sad to say there is no euphonium part in the *Chester Variations for Piano.*

Among the headliners for whom I have played: Tony Bennett, Mel Torme, Al Martino, Dinah Shore, Clay Aiken, Doc Severinsen, Wynton Marsalis, Mercedes Ellington, *Empire Brass, Dallas Brass,* and *The Kingston Trio.* I didn't speak with any of them, but I wish I had. Maybe I could have persuaded one of *them* to write a piece for the euphonium.

Play Like an Egyptian

I finally had the chance to play Verdi's *Aida* at Glimmerglass in 2012. I eagerly anticipated working with the conductor, Nader Abbassi of the *Cairo Opera.* He had already conducted more than 200

---

[39] This is scored for the bassoon and oboe in the orchestral version.

[40] See page 38.

performances of *Aida*, including one that had been televised from the Giza Pyramid.

The run proved to be one of my top ten most enjoyable productions at Glimmerglass. The singing was marvelous, the orchestra was superb, and as for the conducting... In the Disney cartoon version of *The Sorcerer's Apprentice*,[41] Mickey Mouse conducts and all of the objects in the world around him respond to his every gesture. So it was when Maestro Abbassi conducted *Aida,* but without the brooms, buckets, and chaos, of course. Music and emotion seemed to emanate from his hands in a way that I have rarely seen. I would love to play a Puccini opera under his direction, but I can't help wondering if the emotional impact would make it difficult to play.

As we prepared for the final performance, one of the orchestra members came up with an idea for a special tribute to our cherished guest conductor. During the intermission, with the help of a roll of black electrician's tape, we all "grew" an Egyptian goatee a la Maestro's. When we saw the huge grin on his face, we knew he had enjoyed working with us as much as we had enjoyed working with him.

Bass trombone part in Aida. **Is "satanic" redundant?**

---

[41] https://www.youtube.com/watch?v=mHTnJNGvQcA

Random Musings

The voices in my head like it when I have all those measures of rest. Here are some of the things they've said to me.

Hey, if you put a finger in each ear when you sing, you'll sound just like Frank Sinatra. Try it! Oh yeah—it will work best if everyone listening to you also puts fingers in their ears.

Little Debbie's Swiss Rolls should be listed as a controlled substance.

You know, you seem to have your best ideas when you're just waking up or when you're in the shower. Imagine how creative you would be if you added a sprinkler system to your bed!

It's "Pi Day." Why does it seem like it will never end?

They say that running a mile adds 5 minutes to your life. If it takes you 8 minutes to run a mile, you'd actually be losing 3 minutes of life for every mile you run. So *don't* run 10 miles today and live 30 minutes longer as a result.

Taking care of baby boys is as easy as riding a bike: you spend most of your time leaning over, your legs get tired, and if you don't stay alert you *will* get sprayed by something.

I've decided for whom I'm going to vote: the next candidate who responds to an opponent's debate point with "You know, you're right. How can I work with you to make that happen?"

It's true. Hopscotch *is* more challenging if you use real Scotch.

Hey, look at that! Our new Music Director is coming back here to introduce himself to the low brass section. With an attitude like that, this guy will go far! (David Angus at Glimmerglass, now the Music Director at Boston Lyric Opera.)

I like to think that there isn't a moment that goes by without Mozart being performed somewhere in the world.

If I could go back in time, I would take Mozart a computer, printer, MIDI-keyboard, Sibelius music notating software, and a solar powered generator to run them—and hope he didn't waste his time playing computer games.

Whoever invented dogs: *thank you!*

Listening to that "Intermezzo" from *Cavalleria Rusticana* is *almost* enough to make me wish I could play the violin.

Is There a Singer in the House?

Most operas and long-running musicals will designate someone to cover or understudy each of the lead roles. This provides security for the production in the event a singer is indisposed, and it provides other cast members with valuable experience. It might even prove to be the first step toward stardom, as in the case of Sutton Foster's Broadway story come true, when she replaced Erin Dilly in the pre-Broadway run of *Thoroughly Modern Millie* and wound up earning the 2002 Tony Award for Best Leading Actress in a Musical.

Several times a cover at Glimmerglass has been called on to perform, often at the last minute, sometimes even during the performance. I don't recall which opera—and perhaps that is for the best—but I do remember that when one young soprano covered a lead role I actually enjoyed her performance over that of the person she replaced.

During a 1992 performance of Mozart's *The Magic Flute*, the company brought in a substitute singer from New York to sing the role of the Queen of the Night from the pit while the ailing soprano portrayed the role on stage.

For a trombonist, a similar fantasy-come-true might go something like this:

Fantasies Can Come True

As I wrote earlier, *Chicago* has been my favorite band since I first heard their music in 1969. I've bought all of their albums, seen them in concert eight times, and learned to play several of James Pankow's most well-known trombone solos. My second favorite fantasy, behind being the All-Star center fielder and cleanup hitter for the Baltimore Orioles, is to sub one night for James Pankow. Not that I've wasted much time indulging in such fantasies, since both are as unlikely as my third choice, which is to walk on the moon.

In late August of 2013, I heard about *Chicago's* tour date in nearby Schenectady on November 6, a date I had to make, of course. While I sat by the phone in the minutes before tickets went on sale, I figured I'd pass the time by searching the internet for the rest of the tour schedule. I was shocked to find a link to a newspaper article announcing *Chicago's* appearance in Utica, *accompanied by the Utica Symphony!* REALLY? Hey, I'm in that orchestra! But how was that going to happen? The bankrupt orchestra had been out of business for two years. I'm a tenured player, why hadn't I heard of this? I made a couple of quick phone calls, found out it was true, and made sure I got hired.

But it was not to be that easy. Several weeks of "interesting" negotiations ensued between the musicians union and the Utica Symphony Board member who had made the arrangements for the orchestra to play. I won't launder the dirty details in public. Suffice it to say that the Utica Symphony was put on the union's International Unfair List, and we were advised to refuse to play and return the music we had been sent.

If I chose to play the gig in defiance of the union's advice, would I be kicked out of the union? I asked and was told I would not, but I felt certain that if I did play, the majority of my union colleagues would probably hold it against me. I wouldn't blame them a bit, knowing all of the details I haven't shared, but playing in the backup orchestra with *Chicago* would be as close to walking on the moon as I would ever come, surely. Was it worth incurring the ill will of my colleagues and jeopardizing future union gigs to play a dream-come-true concert? Talk about being on the "horns" of a dilemma!

The concert was a few days away. I still had my music. I had not yet responded to the request to refuse the work, even though most of my colleagues had already decided not to play. Several family and friends had already bought tickets to see the show. Could I bear it to sit in the audience and see another bass trombone player in my place? How could I continue to enjoy listening to my favorite band—including several dozen of my favorite songs—if every time I so much as thought about a *Chicago* song I would feel the pain of knowing I had turned down the chance to play with them on stage? After a great deal of soul-searching, I made my decision.

I would play the concert, then resign my tenured positions at Glimmerglass and the Catskill Symphony. It seemed highly unlikely I'd end my career on a higher note. Better to feel like I was going out on top than to walk away after playing a barely significant part in an opera. Besides, I'd purchased a new euphonium earlier in the year, so I could always devote more time to my favorite instrument.

Then I got the joyful news; they had reached an agreement! The tenured members of the Utica Symphony would have first shot at the work, the concert was on. Jason Curly, who had worked hard to keep the gig together, would conduct. (Maestro Schneider was still owed many thousands of dollars by the Symphony and had resigned months before.)

Never had I arrived so early for a gig. As expected, they had the orchestra set up on risers behind the percussion and Robert Lamm's keyboard platform. The iconic *Chicago* horns stood near the front of the stage in front of the trombone section. James Pankow gave us a wave before the rehearsal began and I did my best to avoid gawking like a groupie.

Early on, we rehearsed "If You Leave Me Now," which includes a nice little bass trombone line in the intro. I noticed Pankow watching me from the edge of the stage. After I played that line, he gave me a thumbs up and "golf applause." I've never been prouder to play the bass trombone. Throughout the rest of the rehearsal, he often looked my way to share a joyful smile over the music.

We talked the entire rehearsal break, and he told me to call him "Jimmy." He explained that he had started his study of music at Quincy College as a bass trombone major, then during the summer after his freshman year, he moved to Chicago and booked a lot of gigs with his jazz group. He met reed player Walter Parazaider at DePaul University. Walter recruited him to join the band *The Big Thing*, which was later renamed *Chicago*. None of them had the least idea they would still be together and playing to sold out houses 47 years later, and in that time they have not missed a single concert.

Jimmy told me about the time he wrote the hit ballad, "Colour My World." He had been listening to a lot of Bach preludes and got the idea for the arpeggiated piano accompaniment. Coincidentally, I had spent the summer writing the script for a musical using *Chicago's* music, including some of the obscure classical music from their earliest albums. One of my favorite scenes is where the lead character introduces this new ballad he has written, "Colour My World," to the girl he is falling in love with.

Jimmy said they already had two proposals for musicals on the back burner, yet he graciously took along my script and proposal and promised me their business manager would see it. I'm hoping to get the rights to use the songs so we can mount a regional production. Stay tuned.

The rest of the band was equally as cordial as Jimmy, hanging out during the break and chatting with members of the orchestra. I didn't get to talk to any of the other guys in *Chicago*, though, because I was busy getting to know my new friend.

Me, Jimmy Pankow, Steve Button, Dan Martin

As you can imagine, I've never soaked in every note of a concert as I did this one. My wife, Betsy; my son, Jonathan; and his wife, Kate, were in the audience. My brother, Dan, was able to take a couple of personal days from his high school music teaching job in Pennsylvania to share the moment with me. Two of my best friends, André and Diane French, were also there. I know the orchestra was usually buried in the mix, but that was the night my fantasy came true. I played some of the best brass licks ever written—*with Chicago!*

After the concert, Jimmy called me over, saying, "Put that slush pump to bed and let's talk some more." As enthused as I was to play this one special gig, Jimmy was every bit as psyched about the legacy their band has built, and they are not even close to wrapping it up. They've put together a portable recording studio and recorded eleven new songs in hotel rooms as they toured. Some of the songs have already been released with great success as digital downloads. Their new album, *Chicago XXXVI*, is set for release July 4, 2014. More will certainly follow.

As I made my way out after the show a couple of the orchestra members said, "See you tomorrow night." I had to stop and think. What were they talking about? I was surprised to realize that since I had braced myself for the possibility this might be my last union gig, I had forgotten all about the rehearsal with the Colgate Orchestra and the other rehearsals and concert coming up that weekend.

Now I guess I have to make sure that when the day of that final gig does arrive, it's at least the second best gig I've ever played. Who knows, maybe my final gig will be with *Chicago?* Dreams really *can* come true.

Robert Lamm (keyboard) and the Chicago brass section.

Finale

Well, since you've read this far you have just earned my undying thanks—thank you for indulging me! If you were involved in any of these stories and remember them differently or wish I had included a good story I seem to have forgotten, please email me at LifeInThePitsBook@gmail.com and give me the details so I can include them in the next edition. But if you sell this email address to a spam company, I will hunt you down like the vermin you are! Remember, I have friends in low places. Friends who can infect your digital devices with a charming communicable disease. Speaking of diseases...

I've only missed one performance in my 34-year career at Glimmerglass.[42] I don't recall which opera it was, but between the flu-like crud I'd been fighting for a week and a migraine headache, I had no choice but to call in sick. They did not hire a substitute, probably for two reasons: my part had very few notes that were not doubled elsewhere in the orchestra, and waiting for a sub to arrive may have delayed the curtain.

I will miss two performances on July 26 and 27, 2014 in order to attend the wedding of my son Nathan and his wonderful fiancée Chelsea Katherine Wengler, a very talented actress, singer, and dancer. Coincidentally, their senior years in high school, Chelsea played Belle in Ichabod Crane's production of *Beauty and the Beast* while Nathan played the Beast in Middleburgh's production.[43] Nathan and Chelsea didn't meet, however, until several years later, when Nathan played in the pit for a professional production of *Beauty and the Beast* at Cohoes Music Hall and Chelsea was on stage in the ensemble. I pray their lives will have a similar fairy tale ending. And speaking of fairy tales...

I'll leave you with one of my favorite tales, heard at a Schoharie Valley Concert Band picnic in the 1980s. The person telling the joke gets to select a friend to star in the story, so I will select one of my former students, John Anthony Lopez, a trumpet player who has gone on to develop an outstanding tenor voice. He has appeared many times as a tenor soloist and has starred in many regional theater productions.

---

[42] Due to my previous commitment to direct *Man of La Mancha* in the fall of 2012, I had to decline the opportunity to travel with Glimmerglass to Oman for a one-week run of *The Music Man* at the opulent Royal Opera House in Muscat.

[43] Nathan won an award from Schenectady Light Opera for the special effects he designed and executed in the transformation scene.

John Anthony Lopez could not believe his good fortune. It was like a fairy tale come true! Due to an unexpected illness, he had been called at the last minute to substitute in a trio with Placido Domingo and Josh Groban at Carnegie Hall. He rushed to the rehearsal, unabashedly warming up on the train into town. Joy upon joys, his voice sounded better than ever! He strode on stage, doing his best to hide his nervousness. But just as he reached out to shake hands with his famous colleagues, some rigging broke and an entire rail of lights fell on the three men, killing them instantly.

They awoke to find themselves face to face with St. Peter, standing in front of three closed doors. St. Peter opened the first door and ushered Placido inside while the others watched anxiously from the hallway. Inside the room sat a sore infested, ooze encrusted orangutan. Vermin gnawed at the pathetic creature's feet. A foul stench permeated the air.

A low voice boomed from the heavens, "Placido Domingo, for the sins you have committed on earth, you shall spend all of eternity fending off the romantic advances of this revolting creature." With that, the door slammed shut.

St. Peter motioned to Josh and John to follow and led the way to the second room., The door creaked open, revealing a bubbling cesspool of human and animal filth. A quivering mass of flesh poked its several appendages from the slime, each one grasping hungrily for something to devour. St. Peter shoved Josh Groban into the room and a low voice boomed from the heavens, "Joshua Groban, for the sins you have committed on earth, you shall spend all of eternity fending off the romantic advances of this hideous creature." The door slammed shut.

St. Peter motioned John to follow him to the last door. Well, as you can imagine, John frantically searched his mind for something, anything, that might offer him a chance at redemption.

But it was too late.

The third door creaked opened, revealing Salma Hayek, lying on a sumptuous bed in all of her unadorned glory. Shocked, John looked from Salma to St. Peter, back to Salma, back to—no, he couldn't tear his gaze from Salma. John could not believe his good fortune; this was a fairy tale come true after all!

The door slammed shut and a low voice boomed from the heavens, "Salma Hayek, for the sins you have committed on earth..."

CABARET (Short stories)

My wannabe-writer career began in the Pit of Glimmerglass in 2002. Here are four of my favorite short stories, conceived in the midst of some of the most beautiful musical moments ever written, wonderfully performed by the singers and orchestra of Glimmerglass Opera—and none of which I got to play due to all of those measures of rest.

Hell Hath No Fury...

Springtime in Central Park, so many happy memories! *Ice cream vendors coming out of hibernation... Horseback riding... Roller-skating... Daddy taking her to the zoo (funny how small the zoo seemed now that she was grown.) And her favorite—the swings! Daddy pushing his giggling little girl...*

She settled back into the park bench and smiled, basking in the giggles of her own precious daughter on that very same swing. Instead of her husband, however, the chauffeur did the pushing.

After that disgraceful public debacle and the ensuing exchange of harsh words, her husband had left New York and flown back home without his family. She had decided that they would stay in the city with her mother for a while. Gritting her teeth against a surge of rage, she tightened the blue paisley scarf covering her hair and snugged the dark glasses on the bridge of her nose.

A young couple strolled up the path, picked a spot under a tree about thirty feet from her park bench, spread out a blanket, and sprawled. The boy pulled a transistor radio from his backpack and thumbed it on. The syrupy DJ's voice boomed, "And next up on Sixty-six, Double-you EN Bee Cee: last night's R+B Grammy Winner, Ray Charles, and *Hit the Rooaad Jack!*"

She grimaced, ever so briefly. Her mother's voice rang in her head, as clearly as if she stood behind her. *A lady must never let anyone see what she is thinking or feeling. Smile!*

A dazzling smile filled her visage.

The radio blared, "Hit the road Jack, and don't you come back no more no more no more no more..."

She thought about the irony of the situation. Had it truly come to that point in her marriage? Should she tell her husband to hit the road?

Her daughter's voice rang out from the swings. "Higher! High-Wheeee!"

Her smile broadened, and she thought of her eighteen-month-old son, napping in her mother's apartment over on Park Avenue. He's so much like his father. Her stomach turned. When he grows up, will he be faithless with his wife, too? And like my Daddy? She remembered all too well the pain of her parents' divorce when she was only ten. What would a divorce do to her own sweet children?

The chauffeur waved for her attention. He raised his eyebrows and tilted his head toward the small sliding board. She nodded. He slid the wooden restraining bar up the chains and lifted the four-year old out of the crate-like swing. She was running for the slide before her feet touched the ground.

Despite the joyous scene, her inner storm intensified. *How dare he treat me like that! His one-night stands with anonymous floozies are one thing, but this? The way that slut acted—and with everyone watching!* For nine days the memory of that night had stalked her, looming at the edges of her mind like demons in a Hieronymus Bosch painting.

C.J., her friend since boarding school days in Connecticut, had informed her that among the city's social elite, whispers had turned to open speculation. C.J. went on to suggest that to she should even the score: hire a well-hung pool boy or gardener—or better yet, one of each.

Another friend offered the number for a doctor who could fix her up with a prescription, but she knew too many women who had become enslaved to booze or pills or both to look for solace in that.

One decrepit socialite had the nerve to take her aside at a luncheon and lecture, "Surely you've heard of the seven-year itch. All men stray my dear, but keep your chin up, the smart ones always find their way back home, and your husband is a smart one. You have the children and your charity work to keep you busy in the meantime."

At which she had flashed her smile, but thought, *Men can be cruel, but only a woman could be that vicious.*

A news flash on the radio caught her ear. "...stock market is headed for its worst day since 1919, and will likely close in the 550 range..."

She thought of her former fiancé, a stockbroker. *If I had married him instead, then today would still be a bad day.* Her father had been a stockbroker. And a womanizer...

She took a deep breath, sat up straight, and crossed her legs at the ankles. She laid her hands one atop the other upon her lap. And smiled. Her mother's training once again calmed the waters. Grace. Poise. Elegance. The three cardinal words.

Liar! Deceiver! Bastard! She sobbed—on the inside. In the background, the whining strains of The Four Seasons boomed from the radio. "Big girls don't cry-y-y, they don't cry!"

She sniffed. What do four men know about crying?

She realized she was frowning. Her mother had taught her to chase worries away with happy thoughts. "You don't want to get worry lines when you grow up."

Daydreaming of horses usually did the trick. She recalled her days training for dressage. Her roan was the perfect partner. *What a team we made! Such grace and elegance! One can train a horse, but men? Dogs! Sniffing at any skirt that breezes by.* Her fingernails dug into her palms. *But not my son! I won't allow him to grow up like that!*

An odd creaking sound caught her ear. An oldish woman dressed in nanny's livery waddled toward her, pushing an antique pram. The nanny stopped in front of her. "May I share your bench, Deborah?"

She flinched. How did this woman know about the code name? The man on the phone had told her that due to the sensitivity of the case, he would handle the investigation personally. He had even chosen the code name himself, telling her that her sisters-in-law called her "the deb" behind her back. True, she had been Debutante of the Year, but she never made a big deal about it.

She took a closer look and saw the gleam in the nanny's eyes. Then she noticed the thick make-up, covering what must be a freshly shaven face. "Clever disguise."

"Thank you," the nanny replied, his voice now a gravelly baritone. "I thought it was a good idea. It wouldn't do to have someone see you in the park with a strange man." He took a seat and adjusted the black skirt to cover his knees.

She pictured the nanny waxing his legs—and wished her philandering husband a similar experience in an even more sensitive region of his anatomy. Her smile returned, genuine this time.

The nanny reached into the pram as if adjusting a baby's blanket. "I brought the photos."

The dark glasses slid down her nose as her eyes went wide. Just like that. No small talk. Right to business. Well, better to get on with it; this is hardly the time for social graces. She scooted to the edge of the bench and leaned over the pram. "A real baby?" The infant looked to be about three months old and was sleeping, well, like a baby. She grinned. "C.J. told me you were very thorough with your work, but I had no idea."

"Of course. This business is risky enough. I don't take unnecessary chances." The nanny pulled back the foot of the blanket and revealed a stack of 8x10 black and whites.

Her hand flew to her mouth. She felt as if she couldn't breathe. "I know that place."

"Yes. It is his sister's house." The top photo showed the buxom slut wrapped in a large towel. The shower door stood open in the background.

The nanny moved the photo to the bottom of the stack. The next picture showed her husband, looking over his shoulder as he entered the bathroom. The slut awaited him by the shower.

The next photo was from a different angle. Two naked bodies in the shower.

The nanny started to reveal the next picture.

"Enough." She was too angry to marvel at how he had managed to get such photos. She sat back. She crossed her legs at the ankle. She laid her hands one atop the other upon her lap. She smiled.

But her mind screamed, *I wish he were dead!*

The nanny busied himself rearranging the inside of the pram while she gathered her wits. She turned her eyes upon her precious daughter. She wanted to run and gather the little cherub up in her arms. Maybe hugs would erase the pain, dampen the rage. She ached to hold her children close. She pictured her son, sleeping. The personification of innocence. *I will not allow him to grow up like his father!*

To hell with the scandal. She would divorce the cheating bastard, take the children, and move to Europe. She had always preferred the continent anyway, especially France—not that the men were any better there. She wondered how life would have been different had she disobeyed her mother's wishes and gone back to France to continue her studies.

The nanny's somber voice startled her. "There is more you need to know." His inflection sent a shiver up her spine.

The nanny turned toward her, his mouth ajar as he stared at the young couple, now intertwined on the blanket. His lips barely moved as he spoke. "This woman has become a very loose cannon, and a storm is brewing."

She gulped. "What do you mean?"

"She told two of her friends that your husband is going to divorce you in order to marry her. She is already imagining herself in your place." He paused. "And moving into the house."

Her heart gave one great thud, and then stopped. The smile froze. Life fled her eyes. *And moving into the house.* Her heart jolted back to life, pounding as her pressure soared. Her eyes narrowed. She gritted her teeth and the smile turned to a deadly grimace. Her husband had encouraged her to completely redo the mansion. He knew what the immense project meant to her, how important it was to her to get everything just right. Had he just wanted to keep her busy while he...?

She wanted to run, to find a horse and ride her anguish into the ground. But the problem would still be there, waiting. She stiffened her back. "How much money will it take to make her go away?"

"I'm afraid that won't work, she already has plenty of money. Besides, he has been discussing 'business' with her, which adds more complications. If she told all she knows, she could ruin your husband's business. And then there are the—employees."

She blanched. "Someone has to get through to him! Surely he'll see he must break it off with her. There is so much at stake!"

The nanny adjusted his bosom. "She's fixated on your husband and intends to be his wife. It's all she talks about with her shrink. I don't think she'll give him up. And you know what they say, 'Hell hath no fury like a woman scorned.'"

She scowled. "How do you know all this about her?"

"In my line of work, knowledge is power." He turned and met her gaze.

She saw the glow in his eyes. Her mind raced. And then she understood. He held their future in his hands, and he liked it! She despised him. But in the same moment she recognized her need of such power.

He settled back on the bench. "I see only one solution."

Rage clawed at her soul. Divorce was out of the question now. That would only play into the conniving bitch's hand. If not money, then what? "What solution do you propose?" In the back of her mind a dark thought stirred. She knew the answer before she heard it spoken.

"I can arrange for her to meet with misfortune."

What did that remind her of? King David arranging the death of Bathsheba's husband in order to take his wife. Irony upon irony: her husband had cited the example of David and his numerous concubines to justify his own lecherousness.

"Mommy, mommy, can I get ice qweem?" Her daughter's tiny voice called from the base of the sliding board. The cha-ching, cha-ching of a bicycle bell announced the approaching ice cream cart.

"Yes, sweetheart, you may."

The chauffeur smiled and waved for the ice cream vendor. The little girl's face lit with anticipation as she clapped her hands and bounced up and down.

She pointed to the picture of a Fudgsicle, the chauffeur made the purchase and pulled the wrapper down over the wooden stick to hinder the inevitable finger-seeking drips. Then that first delicious bite. "Yummy!"

How could any decent mother allow such innocence to be threatened by a faithless father and his ambitious tramp? She tucked a stray hair under her scarf, picked up her handbag, and stood. Her tone was as casual as if she had just approved which china should be set out for dinner. "Yes, perhaps that would be best." She smiled, and then left to join her daughter. Every step exuded grace and elegance.

On the radio Gene Pitney crooned,

> *Why do people hurt us so?*
> *Only those in love would know*
> *What a town without pity can do.*

Several days later she returned home with the children. The following weeks passed with varying degrees of tension, and she tried her best to act as though nothing was amiss. She continued to add touches to the house while her husband worked long hours. Their family times were as good as always. Her face never revealed the turmoil seething within.

Then one Saturday morning she came in from the garden and overheard her husband on the phone. "Didn't you go over there to tell her last night?... What happened?... Was she already..." Even from down the hall, she recognized the anguish in his voice. She went back outside to play with the children. Her husband joined them several minutes later. Try as she might, she could discern nothing unusual in his mood or demeanor.

Later, as she approached the kitchen to discuss dinner plans, she heard the cook and a maid as they discussed the shocking news: the slut had apparently committed suicide.

The nanny did it! Good. It's finally over.

She tested her feelings. Any guilt? None. *The bitch has finally reaped what she has sown. Justice is done.*

And most important, her children had been protected.

Her husband was especially tender toward her that night. She smiled her debutante smile and pretended to climax with him, but all the while, the photos she had seen flashed like a torturous slideshow in her mind.

The tension thawed over the next couple of months as she found a dark niche in the recesses of her mind in which to lock away the memory of those photos. Her husband started spending more time with her and the children. Thanksgiving, the children's birthdays, and Christmas passed, happier than ever. By New Year's Eve she was able to again enjoy their lovemaking. And they conceived.

She stood at the hallway window, hands on her bulging belly, admiring the roses in the garden below. Pregnant in summer. Thank God for air conditioning!

But something went wrong.

Labor. Several weeks early.

A baby boy!

A serious respiratory problem.

Two days later she sat propped up in her hospital bed, cradling the feverish infant against her breast. The priest had just left. A nurse checked the flow on the baby's IV, then adjusted the window blinds in advance of the lowering sun's rays.

The tiny boy gurgled. The light faded from his eyes. He went limp in his mother's arms.

No, God, no... Why? Tears welled up in her eyes. She dismissed the nurse. She didn't want to have to play the "lady" during these last few moments with her son.

She placed her thumb in his tiny hand and closed her fingers around his. With her other hand she gently closed his eyes. She leaned over and kissed each eyelid. "Sleep well my precious one." Then she cried as never before.

After the tears ran dry, her chest and head throbbed. Each pulse of her heart sent bursts of pain through her body—and into her soul. She retreated into that place of numbness her mind had created over the years. But a sinister thought followed her there. Remember David and Bathsheba? Didn't their son die on the third day as well?

She sagged. Then wailed.

The nurse burst into the room. "Is everything all right, Mrs.-"

"Get out! Leave us be!"

The wide-eyed nurse fled.

That must be it. God has punished me for my sin—for arranging for that woman's death. How can I ever live with such guilt? She gently squeezed her baby's hand. *Please forgive me, little one. I'm so sorry.* Sobbing, she hugged her son to her heart and begged God to forgive her.

Some time later—minutes? hours?—there came a soft knock at the door. When she didn't answer, the doctor poked his head into the room.

She gave her son one more kiss and hug, then turned her guilt-ravaged face and nodded to the doctor. As he neared the bed, he reached for his stethoscope. She stopped him with a muffled cry and a shake of her head. He gently lifted the baby from her arms and cradled him against his chest. "Your husband should be here in about an hour. His secretary just called."

She didn't care. She wanted to die.

The doctor bowed his head and left, holding the dead infant as if it might break.

She eased out of bed, shuffled to the closet, and lifted her purse from the coat hook. Inside was a bottle of Valium, the newest nerve pill on the market. Since her babies were all bottle-fed, the doctor had insisted she have the drug on hand to fight post partum depression. He had also cautioned her to never exceed the prescribed dosage. Surely the whole bottle would do the trick.

She took the bottle and shuffled to the bathroom, filled a glass with water, unscrewed the little white cap, and dumped the pills into her cupped hand—the one that had just held her baby's hand.

No, Mommy. Don't.

She gasped and whirled in search of the voice. The pills flew from her hand, clattered off the walls, and bounced across the floor like dozens of tiny ping-pong balls.

She strained to listen. There was the electronic hum from the lights. The ventilation system. A droplet of water plopped into the sink behind her. She was alone in the room.

Who?... What?... Baby?... She thought of her living son and daughter. How could she have even considered leaving them behind? She scurried to clean up the pills and flushed them down the toilet. She scrubbed her face, put on her makeup (not bothering with the bloodshot eyes, she'd cover those with dark glasses), and dressed to go home. She packed up her things, and then covered her tousled hair with a scarf, thankful it was not the blue paisley one from that day in the park.

She picked up the phone to call her driver, but decided a cab would be quicker. She slung her purse over her shoulder, grabbed the suitcase, and went to the nurses' station to inform them she was leaving. The head nurse opened her mouth to argue, but evidently thought better of it.

The cab arrived back at the house just as her husband's limo pulled out through the gates and onto the avenue.

Over the following week, despair turned to depression. The sleeping medication only worked for three or four hours at a time. Her husband always came to bed late, even though he had to get to work early each morning. She was well past caring.

The children finally coaxed her outside to the garden. She was helping her daughter draw a picture when the two-and-a-half year old son toddled up with something wriggling in his grimy hands. "Look Mommy, I finded a squirm!"

Her first real smile since before...

Several nights later she awoke and found herself muttering, "Perhaps that would be best. Perhaps that would be best. Perhaps..." She stifled a cry with the back of her hand and rolled over to see if her husband had heard. He wasn't there.

She got up and stumbled into the bathroom for a glass of water, slipped into a silk Cassini robe, then went out into the long hallway to pace. Even though the staff vacuumed the carpet daily, she could still make out the faint path she had worn into the pile over the past week. As she reached the far end of the house, she heard a car drive up.

She pulled back the heavy velvet drape. Her husband's limo sat in the driveway. Light spilled from the house as the side door opened. Two young women emerged, wearing brightly colored, sleeveless shifts—very tight—and high white boots. Her husband came out last. He gave each of the women a lingering kiss, and then assisted them into the limo, fondling them as they sat.

She stepped away from the curtain and staggered back against the wall. *That deceitful bastard! And in this house!* She looked for something to throw at him. The brass planter would do, but it was far too heavy to lift.

Then her eyes grew wide. *My baby didn't die because of my sin! It was for the father's sins after all!* So many late nights "working." The childhood rhyme popped into her mind, mocking her. "All work and no play make Jack a dull boy!"

She raced down the hall to the bedroom and pulled the drawer from her side-table. The contents tumbled onto the floor. She fumbled through the pile, grabbed her address book, and flipped it open to the "J" section. There it was, halfway down the second page: Jed's 24-Hour Cleaning Service, 555-8996. Repeating the number under her breath, she ran into the bathroom and locked the door behind her. She sat on the john, took the phone receiver from the wall, and dialed the number. She cursed the dial as it slowly rotated back into place after the eight and each nine. *They can put a man into orbit around the earth, but no one can invent a fast-dialing phone!*

A perky female voice answered. "Jed's 24-Hour Plumbing Service. To whom may I direct your call?"

She answered softly, "Deborah."

And received the expected answer. "I'm sorry, we have no one here by that name. Perhaps you have the wrong service?"

"Sorry to bother you."

Was that someone in the bedroom? She reached back and flushed the toilet, then hung up the receiver. A few moments later she opened the door.

Her husband sat on his side of the bed. The light from the bathroom glistened on his sweaty face. His brow furrowed. "Can't sleep?" He stood and opened his arms to her.

She turned off the light, took a deep breath, and called on her mother's training for strength. She pasted on a smile, and then went to her husband's waiting embrace.

His cologne was strong. Had he just splashed it on? "Dune pour Homme." She decided it was no longer her favorite. She pulled away, using all her will to keep from retching.

She had to get away from him. She glanced toward the door. "I think I'll go check on the children." Her ultimate source of strength. Her reason for living.

"I'll come, too."

"No." She didn't want him there, fearing his mere presence might infect her son. She struggled to make her voice sound sympathetic. "You must be tired from working so late. I'll just be a moment."

He nodded. Fatigue filled his voice. "I'll wash up."

Heart pounding, she hurried to the children's room.

Her daughter snuggled in a ball under the flannel blanket. One cheek—just a little baby fat left—shone in the beam of light from the hallway.

Her son sprawled across his youth-sized bed. The toes of one foot poked between the bars of the guardrail. His covers clumped at the foot of the bed. She straightened him out and pulled the covers back into place, then rescued Curious George from between the mattress and the wall. The monkey looked much happier with his head on the pillow.

She spent the rest of the night on the rocker in the children's room. And as she rocked, her rage grew.

Fortunately, her husband didn't come looking for her.

C.J. called from New York around noon the next day. After giving condolences about the death of the baby, her voice took on a stilted tone. "Our nanny lost her hat, and she would like me to place an ad in the *Post*." She promised they would get together again sometime soon, and then rang off.

So that was it. The information about her meeting with "the Nanny" would be printed in the "Lost and Found" section of tomorrow's *Washington Post*.

She spent the afternoon napping with her children in the "big bed." Around four, she heard the kids run down the hall, squealing, "Daddy, Daddy!" He was about to leave for his meeting in Chicago. She pretended to be asleep when he came in to say good-bye. He didn't try to wake her, but he did whisper, "I love you."

The children slept with her again that night. She shared half the bed with her daughter; her son spread-eagled on the other half.

They ate breakfast on the patio in the garden. *Cheerios* and bananas. When the children went in to watch Saturday morning cartoons, she hurried to the parlor where the morning papers waited on the coffee table.

She pushed aside the *New York Times,* grabbed the *Post,* pulled out the "F" section, and turned to the "Lost and Found." The ad was about two-thirds of the way down the first column. "Found: Pillbox. Last Sun c.2:00 at zoo near cheetah. 555-8996."

The format was similar to the previous contact in New York. The phone number was the proof. She re-read the ad. Pillbox. Cheetah. The man had a warped sense of humor.

She carefully reassembled the newspaper, locked her problems away in the recesses of her mind, and then went to watch "Mighty Mouse" with her children.

After Sunday Mass, she told her driver to take her to Arlington. The National Cemetery was her favorite hideaway. There was nothing like a long walk through a cemetery to help put things in perspective. She had spent many contented hours touring Robert E. Lee's former mansion and estate, which stood sentinel atop the hill overlooking the graves. She despised the Union soldiers for capturing the magnificent house and burying their dead on the grounds—so the "traitor" could never again call the place home.

The driver pulled up outside the visitor's center at the National Cemetery. As usual, she told him to wait. She didn't know how long she would stay.

She went into the ladies' room and took the stall at the far end. She set her tote bag on the toilet seat and pulled out a pair of flowery clam diggers and a tee shirt. The shirt design featured a rocket blasting off over the words "Mercury 6, First American in Orbit." It was a size too small, which was perfect for her purpose.

She stripped down to her panties. After wriggling into the tight pants, she pulled the shirt over her head and drew her hair back into a ponytail. Makeup darkened her cheeks. She exchanged her Cartier watch for the Timex stashed in the makeup case, then donned a pair of bobby sox and tennis shoes. She tucked the ponytail through the band of a Yankees ball cap and pulled the bill down low. A pair of large, pink-framed sunglasses made the *piece de résistance*. She took her other clothing from the hook on the door, carefully rolled them up, and placed the bundle in the tote bag on top of her pumps, wallet, and makeup case.

She went to the mirror to check her disguise. Not bad—especially the tight shirt with the rocket protruding between her bra-less breasts. Even her husband wouldn't recognize her in such a getup. She felt like a character in an Ian Fleming novel, and fantasized about getting a role as a Bond girl in *From Russia With Love*. She smirked. It was her husband's favorite novel.

She popped two pieces of Wrigley's Spearmint into her mouth, slung the tote bag over her shoulder like a daypack, and went outside. Swinging her hips as she walked, she sauntered out into the bright afternoon sun. Two men in suits and dark glasses looked her up and down. She chomped on her gum, open-mouthed, and ignored them. She flitted right past her driver, who was leaning against the limo. He gawked, but she noticed his eyes never got as high as her chin.

She went to the taxi stand and climbed into the cab at the head of the line. In a heavy Brooklyn accent she said, "National Zoo, if you please." The driver adjusted his rearview mirror to get a better look at her, and then headed for the bridge across the Potomac.

The cabbie dropped her at the Connecticut Avenue entrance. Having been to the zoo several times with her children, she knew the big cats were housed at the other end; but there was plenty of time, it was only 1:31. Just past the ticket booth she stopped and bought a red helium balloon, shaped like the head of a tiger. The face sported a Tony the Tiger grin. The other side proclaimed, "Save the tigers!" She looped the string around her wrist and held the end in her hand. The same hand that had held her baby's hand...

The pent up fury surged through her like a bolt of lightning. If her husband were there, she might have clawed him to death.

Her mother's voice chided in the back of her mind, *Now is that any way for a young lady to act? Control yourself! What will people say?*

But this time, her emotions were too volatile to control. *What about me, mother? Doesn't it matter what I want? Why don't I get a say in anything? Look what my husband did to me—to his family! Don't you care? Look what your husband did to you! And...me...*

She wanted to cry and scream and throw up her hands in despair all at the same time. In a flash of insight, she finally understood Edward Munch's famous painting, "The Scream." It could have been her self-portrait.

Yet the very thought of a work of art calmed her. She imagined herself in happier days, meandering through the Louvre. So much beauty, so much history. Graceful statues. Elegant architecture. Poise. The three cardinal words.

She pulled herself together and bought an ice cream sandwich to soothe her nerves. Thus fortified, she started down Olmsted Walk.

Each step deepened her resolve. She would save her son and daughter. She would not allow their father to mess up their lives as her father had damaged hers.

Even so, she had always adored her father. Why didn't her mother ever lecture him on how a man should act? If she had, maybe he would've behaved himself, and then he wouldn't have had to go away. That was when he started drinking too much. *You were too drunk to give me away at my wedding... You couldn't even attend. Daddy, how could you leave me like that? Why did you cheat on Mommy? Why did you cheat on me!*

She quickened her pace. The balloon bobbed along behind her.

The Great Cat House reeked of urine. Small wonder, she mused. *Their scent is meant to mark a much larger territory than those cages. Maybe I should have "marked" my man. I bet there would be a good market for "Piss sur Homme."*

The cheetahs lived at the other end of the house. Their cage was empty. They must be in their outdoor enclosure. She glanced at her Timex, 1:59.

A Puerto Rican family passed by on their way out of the building. Fluent in Spanish, she struck up a conversation with the mother, strolling with the group as far as the outdoor pens. She kept her eyes out for the Nanny, but couldn't see any likely candidates.

One cheetah dozed on its side under a bush, the other paced back and forth on a well-worn path along the back wall. Its tongue lolled and tail drooped. How could such a magnificent creature look so pathetic?

She unwound the balloon string from her wrist and set her tiger free. Shielding her eyes from the sun's glare, she watched the tiger head soar away, its string swinging like a frisky tail. She hoped that when the balloon drifted back to earth it might find its way into the hands of a lonely child somewhere. But then her mood shifted again. *Knowing my luck, it'll drift into the ocean and find its way into the throat of a dolphin.*

She spent the next half hour pacing in front of the big cats' enclosures. Why didn't the Nanny make contact? Had something gone wrong? Had her husband found out she was up to something? Paranoia struck her like a rogue wave. She was torn between the desire to shrink into the concrete and the urge to run and hide.

A small child's voice rang out, "Lookie! It's Tigger! No—make that two Tiggerrrrs!"

She turned and smiled at the little boy in his green Osh Kosh b'Gosh overalls. The fear subsided, but her knees still felt weak. She found an empty bench and took a seat.

She started to cross her legs at the ankles, then stopped. She slouched on the bench and crossed her arms under her breasts. Getting back into character helped regain her sense of purpose. Then the anger started to bubble, like water just below the boiling point. So she pictured her children, playing in the garden.

Her mother's voice started in on her again: *Sit up str-*, but she squelched that with the memory of grooming her roan after their first win at dressage. The vision vanished at the sound of a man's voice, scolding his obviously over-tired little boy. She nearly lashed out at him. It took every ounce of will to keep her mouth shut, but her mind let him have it with both barrels. *Leave him alone! Don't you dare make him grow up to be like you!*

Then she saw him. He was dressed in drab green, his dingy cap awry. His face hadn't been shaved in a couple of days, and what could have been a handlebar mustache drooped at each end. A dirty canvas bag hung at his side. He used a long-handled pincer to pick up debris, humming as he went. His eyes had the vacant look of a shell-shocked veteran.

She realized he had been working in that area the whole time, but she had never bothered to really look at him. So that was another way to hide in plain sight.

Why hadn't he contacted her? Could it be he hadn't recognized her? She rummaged through the tote bag for another piece of gum, then walked toward the worker, making sure to drop the gum wrappers a few feet in front of him.

As the pincer grabbed the foil, she slapped her head and in thick Brooklynese said, "Oh, I am so sorry. How rude of me. Allow me..." She bent down and picked up the white wrapper. "Here you go, sir." She shoved the paper into his bag.

The worker avoided eye contact, but muttered, "Impressive! I didn't recognize you. Now go to the ladies' room." He bent his head as if looking for more garbage and nodded towards a café, nestled under a grove of trees about forty yards away.

The restrooms flanked the eatery. The ladies' room had three stalls and two sinks. There was a padlocked door at the other end. A janitor's closet? She took the empty stall in the middle and locked the door. Now what? The proximity of the toilet reminded her just how full her bladder had become. She hung the tote bag on a hook and tended to business. Then, remembering a scene from an old movie, she perched on the back of the toilet and rested her feet on the seat.

A minute later she was alone. Someone knocked on the outer door. A gravelly baritone voice called, "Cleaning man. All clear?"

She remained silent. She heard the rattle of keys and a bolt sliding home. Then a whisper. "Deborah?"

She sighed and climbed down. "Here."

"Stay in there." The "janitor" turned on the water in both sinks, then tapped on her door.

Suddenly she felt foolish. What was she doing here? And dressed like that? Was she really going to ask that man to arrange more "misfortune?" How absurd! Was this a Samuel Beckett farce?

A voice in her mind scolded, *Go home woman! You belong with your family. Remember your vows? "Til death do us part."*

She bristled. Was that the voice of her guardian angel? Or an inner demon egging her on? She replayed the admonishment in her mind. When she got to the word "death," her rage erupted. Suppressed images flooded her mind: the debacle in New York, the shower photos, the bimbos in the driveway, her husband as he rationalized his behavior. His face morphed into that of her father, trying to explain why he was moving out—then his besotted face, puking on her wedding day, missing her big event. Big event. The birth of her baby. And his death. *Justice! God, why is there no justice?*

She put her mouth up to the crack in the door. Her voice trembled with passion. "I want him dead."

There. She had said it. And she meant every word of it. The trembling ceased.

The nanny/janitor took a moment before responding. "I thought that might be what this was about. I have to tell you, there are those who want the same thing—though not necessarily for the same reason."

She didn't care. Justice was needed. The time for mercy had long passed. "How much?"

"The others can take care of that. This must never have any possible connection with you." He turned off the water, unlocked the outside door, and left.

She heard the sounds of someone entering the room and quickly resumed her position on the back of the toilet. It took several minutes until the stranger left. Alone again, she climbed down, took her tote bag from the hook on the door, and exited. On the outside of the stall door hung a sign, "Out of service." She tore down the sign and threw it into the trashcan.

It was nearly 4:00 by the time her cab got back to Arlington. She was glad to see that her limo driver had found a shady spot to park. She made a beeline to the visitors' center to clean up and change.

As she neared the limo, her driver jogged up to her, his face frantic with worry. "Are you all right? You were gone longer than usual. A couple of men went looking for you."

She raised a graceful hand to calm him. "I'm fine. I went much farther this time." And every word was true.

Once she stuffed the "worry" into the darkest recess of her mind, she had little trouble settling back into her old routine. Charity work and antique-hunting played second fiddle only to spending time with the children. When in the company of her husband, her smile was her shield. In public she was the model wife. Sleep came easily now—she was confident justice was on the way.

Then her husband had to deal with a particularly troublesome crisis at work. She saw little of him over the next fortnight. He often napped in his office, and when he did go to bed, he fell right to sleep.

The day the problem was resolved, he came to her in the garden, flashing his usual warm smile. He led her by the hand up to their bedroom. She numbed her emotions and closed off her mind, preparing to fulfill her duty.

He locked the door behind them and asked her to sit on the bed. The smile vanished. Worry lines etched his face. He looked ten years older. "I feel like something has happened to me over these past two weeks." He swallowed and cleared his throat. "After coming so close to losing everything—losing the kids—losing you..." Then he fell on his knees before her and burst into tears—great, racking sobs. "I've been so wrong... about so many things... can you please... please forgive me?... I'm so very sorry... I'll never be... unfaithful... to you again." He managed to regain a measure of control. He looked into her eyes. "Can you ever forgive me? Give me another chance? If not for us, then for the kids' sakes?"

She held him while he cried himself out, warning her emotions not to get involved. An old memory wormed its way out of hiding. She saw herself as a little girl, standing outside her parents' bedroom door. Was someone crying inside? Was that her Daddy? Did Daddies even cry? She put her ear to the door. She heard the words "four" and "give" and "chance."

Now she understood.

And yet, a couple of years later her Daddy had left them.

She sat up straight. She crossed her legs at the ankles. She laid her hands one atop the other upon her lap. But the smile would not come.

Her husband looked up at her, eyes pleading.

Was he sincere? No telling what would come out if she opened her mouth. Then again, did it matter at this point? Justice was on the way.

She spoke through clenched teeth. "You killed our baby boy."

His eyes grew wide and his mouth flopped open. He shook his head slowly from side to side. "How can you say such a thing?"

She swallowed hard. "David," tears filled her eyes, "and," she choked on a sob, "Bathsheba." She ran into the bathroom and locked herself in.

Through the door she heard him wail, "Oh God, no! Nooo..."

His muffled cries strengthened her. She gave a small nod. "Justice has begun."

A tiny voice deep within her answered, *But what about mercy?*

Even though her husband had a lot to catch up on after the crisis at work, he still made sure to eat at least one meal each day with his family. They attended Mass together. He even sat down to watch "Disney's Wonderful World of Color" with them on Sunday nights. He went to bed at a reasonable hour—with his wife. He was considerate of her feelings and seemed genuinely interested in hearing about her activities each day.

She found herself wanting to trust him, but didn't dare.

When he told her of his upcoming business trip to Miami, he sounded truly apologetic. He knew she wouldn't be able to go with him, but would she come with him on the next trip, just a few days later? They could attend a luncheon with friends.

Before she had time to think, she heard herself consenting.

When he left for Miami she felt a pang in the pit of her stomach. Did she miss him? Or was it anxiety? How much longer until justice arrived?

Their friends met them at the airport. Some porters saw to the luggage, and the two couples got into a big black convertible. Her husband sat in the back with her, beaming.

She closed her eyes and basked in the mid-day sun. In no time, she was daydreaming about riding her roan—a gentle walk in the meadow. She smiled. Her husband's hand brushed hers, and she didn't flinch. His fingers wriggled between hers and gave her hand a soft squeeze. She sighed.

Perhaps she should call the Nanny and put things on hold.

Maybe the whole thing had fallen through. It had been a while since that meeting, and nothing had happened. Was there still room for mercy?

Weary from the flight but feeling as contented as a well-fed cat, she drifted into that state halfway between sleep and consciousness. She dreamt of riding in the country with her father, but city noises invaded her dream. Her father pointed to an orchard and suggested they help themselves to some apples. To her sleep-fogged eyes the trees looked like people, and the branches waved their arms. *But Daddy, didn't the farmer tell us not to touch the fruit on that tree?*

Her father turned around and said something about "love you"—the rest was gibberish.

She dreamt she picked an apple. Then there was a loud bang. Had the farmer shot at them?

She turned to look. What was her husband doing seated next to her? Two more shots rang out. The side of his head disintegrated. Droplets of blood filled the air. Her mind struggled to distinguish between nightmare and reality. Was that a piece of apple that had flown behind them? She turned and saw a clump of apple atop the trunk of the car. Her husband slumped against her. *I have to get that piece of apple. They will need that to put his head back together.* She crawled over the seat and reached for the apple.

A man in a black suit jumped onto the back of the limo. "Are you all right, Mrs. Kennedy?" The car sped off. Sirens erupted from a pair of motorcycles flanking the vehicle. She slid back into her seat and cradled her husband's shattered head in her lap. Her mind and emotions froze. At the hospital, she handed a doctor the clump of brain tissue she had retrieved from the trunk lid.

And then the nightmare became reality.

****

Author's note: This story is in the "alternate history" genre. I do not wish to cast any aspersions upon the character of Jackie Kennedy. I don't believe she would ever have acted in many of the ways this story portrays. She truly deserves her revered place in history, and I apologize to anyone who may take offense, there is none intended.

The very nature of "alternate history" is to explore the possibilities—the "what ifs" of well-known historical events. Many things mentioned in this story are documented and true. Most of the fun in reading an alternate history comes from following the interplay of fact and fiction. Perhaps the most tragic fact in this story is Mrs. Kennedy's retrieval of the piece of her husband's head, and then giving it to a doctor at Parkland Hospital (as related in the Warren

Commission Report.) I wouldn't dare make up such a grisly detail.

The premise for the story was inspired while watching the Glimmerglass Opera performance of Poulenc's one act opera, *Le Voix Humaine*. It is a one-woman show, the story of a woman at the end of an affair. The libretto consists of her side of telephone conversations with the lover who has dumped her. Through the course of the hour the audience follows her declining psychological condition. The woman is a well-to-do, buxom, platinum blonde. At one point she dons a pink dress. I guess it was the juxtaposition of the buxom blonde—Marilyn Monroe's trademark—and a pink outfit, forever etched in the American psyche as Jackie Kennedy's attire on that tragic day in Dallas, that set my mind working in the direction this story has taken.

A half hour spent "Googling" for background facts revealed a goldmine of material for an overactive imagination... And don't we all enjoy playing armchair psychologist now and then?

7/31 - 8/9/2005

TRUTH vs. FICTION in "Hell Hath No Fury..."

There is a wonderful little zoo in Central Park's southeast corner, founded in 1864, modernized in the 1980s.

Jackie Bouvier's father often took her to the park, the zoo, out for ice cream, etc. She grew up in a Park Ave. apartment and went to boarding school in Connecticut.

The "public debacle" mentioned was the infamous rendition of "Happy Birthday" sung by Marilyn Monroe to JFK during his birthday celebration at Madison Square Garden on 5/19/62. She had to be sewn into the sheer slip she wore. Their affair is reputed to have begun as early as January 1962.

The AM radio station, WNBC (660 on the dial) used to have a pop format. (Today it has a sports format.)

Ray Charles' "Hit the Road Jack" won the Grammy award for R&B on 5/27/62. "Big Girls Don't Cry" and "Town Without Pity" were also big hits in 1962. (Thus the date of the opening scene is 5/28/62.)

Jackie's mother was reputed to have been very controlling, and taught her the social graces. She divorced "Black Jack" Bouvier when Jackie was ten. He was a stockbroker and a womanizer.

Hieronymus Bosch (1456-1516) was a painter of surrealistic, fantastic religious scenes, horrifying in many details. Check him out on line (but not on a dark, stormy night alone.)

C.J. is NOT based on any real character. However... Jackie's sister was named Caroline, and, of course, her children were Caroline and John—so that was one reason for using those initials. One of my friends acquired the nickname C.J. (for Cracker Jack—don't ask), and on several birthdays past she has called to wish me happy birthday, singing "Happy Birthday Mr. President" in her best Marilyn Monroe imitation. She does not have a pool boy or a gardener.

Marilyn Monroe's most famous movie was "The Seven-year Itch" and includes the scene where her white dress blows up around her waist as she stands on a subway vent. Thus Jackie's thought about how only a woman could be so vicious as to open a supposedly consoling conversation with a reference to a movie starring the woman who was having an affair with her husband.

The stock market took the specified dive on 5/28/62.

Jackie was first engaged to a stockbroker.

Jackie loved horses and dressage. By the time she was eleven she had already won several national championships.

Jackie's sisters-in-law called her "the deb" behind her back. She was NYC's Debutante of the Year, 1947.

Leg waxing dates from the 1930s, and was first called a "European Wax" since it originated in European spas.

The incident in the shower: no photos were taken that I know of, however, such incidents reputedly took place at the home of Peter Lawford, married to JFK's sister.

Jackie studied at the Sorbonne and was a Francophile. Although she won the opportunity to do an internship in Paris, she turned it down, honoring her parents' wishes.

Marilyn Monroe told people she expected JFK to divorce Jackie and marry her. She privately spoke of her dream of being First Lady.

Jackie did a wonderful job restoring the White House and saw it as a national monument. On Valentine's Day 1962 she gave a televised tour of the White House, which had been seen around the world. Thus, I believe she would have been outraged had she known of JFK's numerous trysts with women under that roof.

J. Edgar Hoover is reported to have had wiretaps indicating JFK discussed government matters with Marilyn. "Employees" refers to U.S. citizens.

Near the end of her life, Marilyn saw her shrink on a daily basis.

The circumstances surrounding Marilyn Monroe's death have been fodder for all kinds of theories. Suicide, accident, or murder? Witnesses reported seeing Bobby Kennedy in the vicinity that night. One source holds that JFK sent Bobby to tell Marilyn that the affair was over. Thus, my fictional one-sided phone conversation is between JFK and Bobby. The official coroner's report lists suicide as the cause of her death. But who ever committed suicide by means of a barbiturate enema?

The garden in the story is the famous Rose garden at the White House.

Jackie went into premature labor with her son, Patrick. He died of a respiratory ailment on the third day. Valium was new on the market in 1963. All other details in that regard are imagined. (And I imagine she would be one of the few people with enough clout to discharge herself from the hospital.) The location of the hospital was changed from Boston to D.C. for the convenience of the storyline. JFK was at that hospital, the location of a unique breathing chamber. The baby died at 4:04 AM.

Jackie loved French designers, but once she became First Lady she decided it best to "buy American." Oleg Cassini was her top choice among American designers.

Jed's Plumbing Service: The name Jed is in "honor" of J. Edgar Hoover—as is the appearance of a man dressed as a woman. (There is no reliable proof that he ever dressed as a woman.) Some conspiracy theorists link the FBI and/or the CIA to JFK's death. This plays into that theory. I have no opinion, but wanted to leave the possibility of such a connection open in this story. (And those who later broke into the Watergate Hotel were called "the plumbers.")

The phone number: 8996 are the last four digits for my office number. And remember those old rotary dial phones, and how the dial seemed to move even slower when you were in a hurry?

"Dunne pour Homme" was one of the first cologne's marketed for men. "Piss sur Homme" was not, though no doubt some women might want to use it on their men.

In the lost and found ad, "pillbox" refers to Jackie's favorite kind of hat, the type she wore on 11/22/63. "Cheetahs," of course, is a bad pun on "cheaters.""

There were newspapers named "Post" both in NY and Washington.

The history of Robert E. Lee's estate is true.

Mercury 6 blasted off on 2/20/62 from Cape Canaveral (renamed Cape Kennedy after the assassination.) John Glenn was the first American to orbit the earth. The flight lasted just under five hours. JFK galvanized the U.S. and NASA to put the first man on the moon by the end of the decade. (Arguably his greatest legacy.)

From Russia With Love was released in England in 1963, the US in 1964. JFK told *Life Magazine* in 1961 that it was his favorite James Bond novel. Jackie was a very beautiful woman and was a very rebellious teen at boarding school. I wouldn't be surprised to learn that at one time she actually behaved as I portrayed her in that scene, though I can't imagine any First Lady doing that. (She hated the term "First Lady"—said it sounded like the name of a horse!)

The two men in suits and dark glasses were Secret Service men assigned to protect the First Lady. That was the main reason for her elaborate disguise, etc. (And the "nanny's" disguise.)

Jackie was fluent in Spanish and French, and having grown up in NYC she could have been very adept at "Brooklynese."

The current layout of the National Zoo has a Cheetah exhibit right inside the Connecticut St. entrance. The Great Cat exhibit is at the other end of the zoo. I don't remember the zoo's layout in the 1960s, but recall that "free-ranging" exhibits were not yet common. Most of the animals had an indoor cage with a hatch opening into a small outdoor enclosure.

I had that red tiger balloon in the early 1960s.

Sadly, Jackie's father was too drunk to even attend her wedding.

Pablo Casals, one of the world's great cellists, performed at the White House on 11/13/61. His very emotional encore was this folksong.

Jackie loved her children and protected them as much as possible. She was often characterized as shy and private. Her parents' divorce and her husband's infidelities must have had a detrimental effect, thus the armchair psychoanalysis leading to my portrayal of the eruption of her repressed feelings.

Edward Munch's *The Scream* popped into my mind as I wrote the associated scene; that was when I truly understood the painting. The Kennedy's were great patrons of the arts, primarily due to Jackie's love for them.

"Osh Kosh b'Gosh" has been around since 1895, and starting making kid-sized overalls about twenty years later.

Samuel Beckett (1906-1989) was one of five dramatists at the center of the "Theater of the Absurd" movement. *Waiting for Godot* and *Endgame* are his two most well known plays.

The "particularly troubling crisis at work" refers, of course, to the Cuban missile crisis. This was perhaps the closest the world has ever come to all-out nuclear war. Many people took a closer look at their priorities during that time. My uncle served on the USS Enterprise (aircraft carrier) during the blockade of Cuba. His captain was not named Kirk. (Watch the movie *Thirteen Days.*)

Unless you grew up without color TV, you can't imagine what a treat it was to be invited over to a friend's house to watch TV in color on Sunday nights: the NBC peacock opening its colorful tail, then Disney, followed by "Sing Along with Mitch." (Suggest a TV sing-along for broadcast today and see what happens?)

JFK went to Miami 11/19/63. Jackie went with him to Dallas on the 22nd. They rode in a limo with Texas governor John Connally and his wife. Shortly before the fatal shots, Mrs. Connally turned and said, "Mr. Kennedy, you can't say Dallas doesn't love you now." Thus the source of the words "love you" in this story.

The nightmare of her father encouraging her to take an apple from the tree with forbidden fruit is an allusion to the Biblical account of Eve's sin. More amateur psychobabble: On the one hand, I see her adoring her father, with possibly an element of an Elektra complex, shown when she wonders why her Daddy had betrayed her. On the other hand, her anger towards his behavior and moving out (abandonment issues) would cast him as a devil.

As previously mentioned, after the shots Jackie saw a piece of her husband's head atop the trunk of the car, which is why she crawled over the back seat. It has been reported that on the way to the hospital she repeatedly said, "I have his brains in my hand." She gave the piece to a doctor at Parkland Hospital.

And I hope you picked up on my various attempts at irony in the story. The closing sentence is foremost, when her nightmare becomes reality—a reality that is even worse than the nightmare.

JFK was buried in Arlington National Cemetery on 11/25/63. Patrick was reinterred there. Jackie was buried next to JFK on 5/23/94.

To end on a positive note: after JFK's funeral the *London Evening Standard* reported, "Jacqueline Kennedy has given the American people...one thing they have always lacked: majesty."

This next story was written for a short story contest. There were two requirements: be set in an alternate universe or reality and be no longer than 500 words.

All for the Want of a Horseshoe Nail

"Mama, I'm hungry! How long 'til dinner's ready?"

"Go play with your brothers, Adler. I'll call you when it's ready."

The youngster crinkled his nose and snorted. "I'm bored! And hungry! Why don't you make the fire hotter?"

The mother looked up from her cooking and gave a weary smile. "You know the old saying, 'A watched pig never broils.' Besides, your Papa doesn't like his pork scorched."

Adler scuffed dirt towards the fire pit. His mother sighed. "Go ask Papa to tell you a story. I'll call you-"

"Adler, come here!" It was Papa, standing near a tall oak at the edge of the cornfield. Adler's two younger brothers perched on a fallen trunk.

Adler flew to his father's side. "Papa, tell us the story about Great-great-grandfather and the mighty knight. Pleeease?" His brothers leapt to their feet and joined in a whiny chorus. Papa waved for quiet and his sons sat, their eyes glowing with anticipatory delight.

A gentle breeze ruffled the cornstalks. The alluring aroma of roast pork wafted by. Papa grimaced and ignored the low, hungry grumble in his belly. He filled his voice with drama and began the tale.

"It happened on the isle of Silene, many years ago. Your Great-great-grandfather, Brandeis the Magnificent, was stag hunting when he came upon a mighty knight atop a pure white warhorse.

"The knight threw open his visor and shouted, 'I challenge thee this day to single combat—to the death!'

"Brandeis scoffed. 'What would thou have do with me? I know thee not.'

"The brash young knight persisted. 'Is it my name thou lackest? Or courage? I am George of Cappadocia. So now, where be thy courage?' His warhorse pawed the ground. His armor sparkled in the sunlight.

"Brandeis retorted. 'I would not engage thee in unequal combat.'

"The knight loosed an angry roar. 'Defend thyself!' And with that, he slapped his visor shut and charged.

"Brandeis stood tall and braced for the attack. The warhorse's hooves thundered across the hard ground. The knight's lance dropped into attack position. Sunbeams glinted off the shiny armor and into Brandeis' eyes, but he dared not avert his gaze."

Papa paused. Adler hunched in dread, his brothers sat wide-eyed and breathless.

"The charging destrier was but five yards away when one of its shoes came loose, spun forward, and caught on the ground. The horse stumbled. The knight's lance tipped downward. It gouged Brandeis' leg! Blood spurted everywhere! Brandeis lunged for the knight. And with one gulp—he swallowed him whole!"

Cheers and hurrahs greeted the happy outcome.

Papa cocked his head and the siblings quieted. "Thus is the tale of Brandeis the Magnificent and the martyr St. George, as the humans have since named him."

Mama screeched in the distance. "Dinner!"

The hungry young dragons squawked and flew to the fire pit, where a dozen perfectly roasted hogs awaited them. Papa cast a proud glance at the smoldering ruins of the nearby farm, spread his wings, and joined the repast.

Many of the details in this next story are from my personal experiences.
Lohra is not one of them.

Lohra

She said her name was Lohra. At least, that was the way it
sounded as the syllables oozed from her pouty lips. Her accent was
some wondrous combination of French and German. She said she
had grown up in the Rhine river valley. Lohra. Laura?

Laura was my grandmother's name. I wanted to name one of
my daughters Laura, but my wife didn't care for it—said it was too
old-fashioned. Old-fashioned? Another proof of my lack of style, I
guess; but I've always liked that name, even the way it feels to say it.
Laura. That is, until I met Lohra. And the way she added that sultry
breathlessness between the syllables.

Lohra. The enchanting sound of her voice. Those glorious
golden tresses, springing from her head as if it was the source of all
hair: cascading around her ears, draping across her shoulders,
flowing down her arms, framing her perfect breasts—

I shook my head to regain my composure, reached down, and
pried my carry-on bag from under the seat in front of me. I zipped it
open and removed my travel wallet from the inside pocket. I had to
see the picture of my family! I nudged the bag halfway back under
the seat with my foot and flung the wallet open with all the fervor of a
drowning man gasping for air. My elbow bumped the elderly German
woman seated next to me. "Entschuldigen Sie bitte, gnadige Frau." I
knew *gnadige Frau* was a bit archaic, but I presumed she would
appreciate the gesture.

The woman beamed. Wrinkles streamed from the corners of
her sparkling blue eyes like rays of sunlight. "Certainly. How nice to
hear an American speak German, and with such good manners."

"Thank you, and your English is excellent." I surveyed her
crinkled face, hoping to purge the image of Lohra from my mind. It
didn't work. Lohra, how I long to see you... I gulped. The picture!

The old woman probably reconsidered her initial impression of
my politeness as I thrust the photograph in front of her eyes. "Would
you care to see a picture of my family?" Just as quickly, I pulled it
away and pointed out my children. "This is my oldest daughter,
Anna; my son, Benjamin; and our youngest, Cynthia. And that is my
wife, Loh-, uh, Lisa." Lisa... Loh- LISA!

"What a nice looking family you have. And such a beautiful
wife. You must be very happy." She reached over and patted my arm
much like my grandmother used to do, then turned and looked out
the window.

My grandmother, Laura. Lohra. LISA! I flipped to the next
picture—Lisa and me on our twentieth anniversary. I gazed into her

eyes and basked in the memory of that weekend at the cabin on Lake George. What we did in the cabin. And in the woods. And in the lake. I took a deep breath and let it out very slowly. It reminded me of the Lamaze classes we took when Lisa was pregnant with Anna. What a little sweetheart, that Anna.

At the very edges of my consciousness, a more recent memory lurked, seeking a way to sneak past that meddlesome love for my family. I closed my eyes and lay back in my seat. My fingers caressed the photo as if the action might somehow summon the image of Lisa before me. It was working. As thoughts of Lisa filled my mind, the siren call of what's-her-name faded. I remembered the day I first met Lisa at a showing of the classic movie *It Happened One Night*. Ithaca College. We went for a walk around the pond and talked long into the night...

Exhausted from my trip, I slipped into that half-awake state that passes for sleep on an airplane.

I rarely traveled alone, but as the new sales manager at Albany Porsche/BMW, I was required to attend a conference at the Porsche plant in Stuttgart. As in Stuttgart, Germany. Spouses were not invited. What was I to do? Fortunately, I have the world's most understanding wife. And I promised her another trip to Lake George. Talk about a win-win situation! Not only did I get to go to Europe, I got to look forward to another romantic weekend with my wife.

The Porsche plant was amazing, but in a surprising show of paranoia we were sworn to secrecy about the details. And no photos!

The conference ended and we had a day to ourselves for sightseeing. I was anxious to try out my German: to stave off boredom on slow sales days, I had often listened to German language instruction CDs at my desk. I had always been fascinated with the Alpine countries and several of my customers were of German heritage, so I figured the ability to speak some German wouldn't hurt my chances of closing a few extra sales. I was right. It also garnered me lots of referrals and eventually, the position as sales manager.

I rented a car and headed south for Lake Konstanz. It was a gorgeous day for a drive; sunlight streamed through meandering clouds in the silken sky. The ebony BMW hummed along the autobahn at 160 KPH. I did some quick mental math and realized that I was going just under 100 MPH. I pushed it up to 170...180...190...200. That car could really purr. (Or was it me?) When I die, I hope the undertaker will make my smile just the way it must have been at that moment.

The red-circled signs outside of Ravensburg announced a speed limit of 120. The highway passed through the city and headed down into the valley towards Friedrichshafen and the Lake. That was when I spotted the blimp. It was white with Zeppelin NT emblazoned in blue letters across its side. I recalled reading that Graf von Zeppelin had lived and worked in Friedrichshafen. I moved over to the right hand lane and cast careful glances skyward. I had seen the Goodyear blimp flying over Schenectady several years ago, and this one was maybe half the size of that. Its gondola had several windows. Did they offer rides to the public? It slowly descended towards the outskirts of the town. I decided to follow it.

Do you ever take the time to look back over your life at some of the decisions you've made? Strange, isn't it? How often the most innocuous choices could have the most devastating consequences.

I lost sight of the blimp, but followed the signs to the *flughafen*. Biting back my male pride, I pulled up to a Polizei car, pushed the button to open the passenger-side window, and asked, "Koentten Sie mir sagen, wo kann ich der Zeppelin finden?" I didn't know for sure, but I presumed the German word for blimp was zeppelin, what with the Hindenburg and all.

The officer smiled and answered in Arnold Schwarzenegger English. "They have their own airfield. Take the next roundabout and head back the way you came. Turn right at the next crossroad and follow the fence on your right. It will lead you to the field."

I was too excited to struggle with any more German syntax, and his English was clearly better than my German, so I blurted, "Is it possible to get a ride on a blimp there?"

The officer turned to his partner and they laughed. I felt like JFK must have on that infamous day in Berlin when he learned he had called himself a jelly donut. "Ich bin ein Berliner."

The officer turned back to me with a smirk on his face. His tone was curt. "Yes, they give rides, but maybe not if you call their zeppelin a blimp. Their airships are zeppelins. A blimp is nothing but a big balloon." He sounded like Arnold talking about "girlie men."

I pointed to my head, the universal sign for *I'm an idiot.* "Thanks for the tip!" Then I drove off in quest of the zeppelin.

As I rounded the last turn along the fence, I saw the Zeppelin NT building on my right. The white zeppelin slowly descended behind it. The road ended in a parking lot in front of the building surrounded by a chain link fence. In front of that was a large white tent with a sign: *Eingang.* Enter.

I parked the car, grabbed my camera, tucked my travel wallet into the inside pocket of my jacket, and dashed for the entrance. It was only forty yards, but I panted as if I had run a mile.

A young man and woman stood behind a curving glass counter filled with zeppelin souvenirs. A quick glance around showed a bar to my right and about a dozen people standing just outside the opposite side of the tent, gawking at the ground crew as they moored the floating airship.

"May I help you?" The young woman's English was superb. How did she know I spoke English? I tried so hard to not look touristy.

I hurried over to the register. "Is it possible to purchase a ride on the zeppelin?" Despite my best efforts, my face must have been wrenched with anxiety, fearful of a negative reply.

The woman smiled. "You are in luck, sir. We have had a cancellation and there is one seat available." She turned and grinned at her partner as I exhaled with relief.

I pulled out my wallet. "American Express?" It was all I dared say. I was afraid I'd start babbling. I loved flying. It was a sunny day. And I was already imagining the spectacular views of Lake Konstanz, the Bavarian Alps to the east, the Black Forest to the west, and those incredible Swiss Alps to the south.

The man's brow wrinkled. "Don't you want to know how much it costs?"

"Does it matter?" As I signed my name on the *unterschriffen* line, I saw the fare: 390 euros. Unbidden, my mental calculator went to work. At $1.18 per euro, that was about $460.00! How would I explain that expense to Lisa? Well, this was my once in a lifetime chance to ride on a zeppelin—I had to do it. Besides, how could Lisa retain her title as World's Most Understanding Wife if I didn't give her a challenge now and again?

The man handed me my receipt and a boarding pass. "The others have already received their flight instructions. I will go over them with you. Walk this way." I followed the limping young man

over to a bulletin board, resisting the urge to mimic his gait a la Gene
Wilder in *Young Frankenstein*.

The board showed how to don a life jacket, and the man
quickly explained how the ground crew would lead the twelve
passengers out onto the airstrip. We were to wait, single file, until we
received the signal to board the ship one at a time. "The zeppelin is
hovering over the ground and is restrained by guide-wires. We don't
want more than one person on the gangway if a gust of wind happens
along at the wrong time."

I nodded my understanding and pointed to the passengers
who were boarding a van. "Do I need to—"

"Yes. Let's hurry." The man led me through the tent flap and I
made it to the van just as they were getting ready to close the door. I
ducked my head and claimed the vacant seat in the back.

"Wilkommen meine Damen und Herren..." I tuned out the
pre-recorded welcome and gazed past the other passengers at the
airship, floating several feet above the ground.

Out of the corner of my eye I saw her.

My mouth dropped open.

My heart skipped a beat. Or four.

She was sitting at the other end of the seat in front of me,
next to the window. Her blonde hair—or should I say Blonde hair, it
was that perfect—shimmered with the sun's backlighting. She turned
to the front and I saw her cheek, a delicate mound of— My face
flushed. I gripped the edge of the seat. I was glad I was not sitting
within reach of her. I felt the most incredible urge to ever so gently
caress that cheek. To see if it was real? No... To understand the true
meaning of the word *soft*.

The van eased to a stop. I wrenched my eyes from the woman
and stared down at my trembling hands. My fingers dug into the
vinyl upholstery. The door opened. A cool breeze entered. I snorted
softly and relaxed. Boy, I sure do miss you, Lisa! I wish you were
here! In more ways than one...

A member of the ground crew told us to line up according to
our boarding pass numbers, starting with row six in the back. That
was me. I kept my eyes on the airship, bobbing gently against its
moorings. I was about to fly in a zeppelin! The adrenalin rush was
just the diversion I needed to push the Blonde's image from my mind.
The hum of the engines deepened as the pilot made adjustments to
keep the zeppelin level. The propellers on both forward engines
pivoted upward, pushing the zeppelin down. The tailfin slowly moved
left and right as needed, directing the air from the rear prop to
counteract the crosswind. Oddly, it made me think of a hooked fish,
resisting the urge to struggle free.

I got the signal to board and strode for the gangway. As instructed, I reached for the railing on both sides, climbed up onto the bottom step, then proceeded up the stairs and into the cabin. Six rows of paired seats went down the middle of the gondola. A stewardess showed me to my seat and reminded me to fasten my seat belt right away. I quickly buckled in, took an eager breath, and looked up. Somehow I think I already knew.

The Blonde strode down the aisle. The slit in her knee-length black skirt flashed a tantalizing glimpse of her well-tanned thighs. Her light blue turtleneck sweater clung to her spectacular body as if it was scared of flying. She wasn't wearing a bra. (Before you call me a pig, understand that I had quickly glanced away, but her image had already seared itself into my synapses.)

She sat next to me. Her hand brushed my thigh as she reached for her seat belt. It felt like a bolt of electricity shot through my groin. In reflex, I turned and faced her. I can't imagine the expression on my face.

Her moist lips parted. "Hello, my name is Lohra."

I love music. In fact, I'm a pretty good amateur musician – if you believe tuba players can aspire to such things. I love a good Beethoven symphony (redundant, I know), and I used to think Charlotte Church had an amazing voice. But that was before I heard Lohra speak. I already mentioned her accent, but from the timbre of her voice and the lilt of the words— "You must be a singer."

She smiled and blushed. My heart melted.

Remembering my manners, I started to offer my hand, but then slid it under my leg. I didn't dare touch her. "My name is Jason." I wanted to add, "It's a pleasure to meet you, Lohra," but I didn't want to profane the air with my feeble imitation of the perfection with which she had pronounced her name.

"Yes, Jason, I am a singer. How did you know?"

I was never so happy that apparently everyone in Europe could speak English. "Your voice. It's, well...so musical. I'd love to hear you sing sometime."

"Thank you." She glanced down and her blush deepened. Her pink cheek beckoned my touch. I gripped my leg as if it was the edge of a cliff. Then her deep blue eyes met mine. "But I'm on holiday. I don't plan to sing any more until I return home. You'll just have to come visit me."

I had seen plenty of beautiful women before—heck, my Lisa was just about as beautiful as any man dared hope to marry. But Lohra was challenging the English language's ability to describe beauty. Not to mention sexy. In my twenty-one years of marriage I had never strayed. I knew every man had his limits. I now knew mine.

I knew what I had to do. It was my only hope.

Reaching inside my jacket, I pulled out my wallet. "Would you like to see a picture of my family?"

I had only been seriously tempted on two other occasions in my life. Pulling out my family picture had been the perfect life preserver. This brewing tempest would surely put that measure to the test.

Much to my relief, Lohra oohed and aahed over my pretty daughters and my strapping son. I put the wallet on my lap, with the picture showing. I needed Lisa's smiling face to stiffen my resistance to Lohra's captivating voice and personality. We chatted about our homes and I learned she had left Germany some years ago, and now lived on a tiny, uncharted island off the coast of Florida. She had come back to visit her father, but would leave soon to return to her island. She much preferred the warmer climate. She liked to swim in the nude.

The zeppelin finally took off amidst the roar of its engines and the enthusiastic applause of the other passengers. The sounds barely covered my groan as I imagined Lohra frolicking in the waves.

I stared out the window as the airship drifted up and angled toward the lake. It took only a few minutes to reach cruising altitude of a thousand feet.

The view was beyond what I had imagined. My eyes feasted on the snow-capped Alps to the south. It was difficult to distinguish between the mountaintops and the banks of billowing clouds. "Someday, I will bring my skis and we will have at it!" I vowed softly.

"What?"

Lohra's breath moistened my ear. I shivered and turned. Lohra's hair brushed my cheek as she backed away just in time to avoid bumping heads. I grasped for my wallet and stared down at Lisa's face. I could have sworn her expression turned to a glare. I blinked. Hard. Good, Lisa's smile was still there.

"Lisa and I love to ski. I can't wait to take her skiing in the Alps someday." Actually, Lisa was terrified of heights. I know she'd never get on a ski lift, and her cross-country skis have only been used twice. But I had to keep my mind on Loh-...LISA.

Lohra pulled her hair back behind her ear so as not to block her face. "I prefer the water. Growing up on the river as I did, I just don't feel at home unless there's water near by." The plaintive tone in her voice made me want to go right out and get her a whole lake full of water.

A voice came on over the intercom. There was an announcement in German, repeated in English, "The captain has turned off the seat belt sign. You may now feel free to get up and move about the cabin."

Lohra quickly undid her belt. Her hand again brushed against my thigh. Then she gave me a knowing smile, stood, and moved to the large window behind us, which looked eastward over the walled island-town of Lindau. The Bavarian and Tyrolean Alps sprawled beyond. I waited a moment for my pulse to slow, put away my wallet, and then moved to the front of the ship. I needed to distance myself from you-know-who.

I spent several happy minutes watching the pilot and co-pilot maneuver the controls. Next to me was a large window, slanted outwards, which gave a view directly below. I pulled out my camera and commenced shooting like a pro—the camera's 512 MB flashcard could easily store over 300 pictures. I got shots of the rippling lake, dozens of brightly colored sailboats in a regatta, the shadow of the zeppelin on the water, and zoomed in for some stunning shots of the Swiss Alps. The zeppelin started a slow turn as we headed back down the lake. I stayed at my post and shot the town of Lindau, its ancient lighthouse, and the Thieves' Tower. I even got a picture of the Bregenz Festival Theater, its stage built on the lake. A stewardess told me they were preparing for an upcoming production of *West Side Story*. My luck, I finally got to Europe and they were playing an American musical.

The announcement came on advising us to return to our seats. As I weaved through the other passengers I saw Lohra standing in the aisle, a man bent over her hand, his lips pressed against her flesh. The man straightened and I heard him mutter, "...*bella dona.*" Jealousy raged within me.

Before I could act, a portly woman rolled her eyes and grabbed the man by the arm. "Enrico!" She dragged him back to their seat in the fourth row.

I stepped past the couple and moved to my seat. The stewardess in the back eyed my camera. "Would you like me to take your picture?" She nodded to the seat in front of the large rear window. The zeppelin had turned again and Lindau was framed perfectly.

Lohra and I spoke at the same time. "Yes, I'd like that."

I gulped. Lohra quickly perched on the bench. She looked up at me expectantly and patted the seat next to her. I handed the camera to the stewardess and moved numbly to Lohra's side.

"Smile!"

I swear I *felt* Lohra smile.

I must have looked like a deer in headlights.

The stewardess handed me the camera and somehow my legs carried me back to my seat. Lohra eased in next to me. This time her hand did not make contact with my thigh. I was scrunched as close to the far edge of my seat as I could go. I slipped the camera into my pocket, groped inside my jacket to retrieve my life preserver, and opened to the anniversary picture. Was Lisa frowning? I blinked.

"Well, Jason, I guess you'll need my address if you want to come to my island to hear me sing." Lohra reached for her purse and pulled out a notepad and pen. Her hand flowed across the paper with the grace of a prima ballerina. She folded the paper in half, reached over, pulled back the corner of my jacket, and tucked the paper inside my shirt pocket. She patted it for good measure. I wondered if the sensation was anything like the jolt from a defibrillator. My resistance evaporated. I had to have this wondrous creature. I would give anything, if only—

Lohra's musical tone washed over me. "And please bring your family."

That word saved my life.

Family.

The thought of my family broke the spell and allowed me to tear my eyes from hers. I looked down. Lisa beamed up at me. Her smile reminded me of her teary look as we stood before the minister during our wedding. I closed my eyes and leaned back in my seat. My ears rang. I imagined them to be the church bells as we dashed down the steps, birdseed and rice raining upon us. The car door slammed shut. I heard the voices of well-wishers as the driver whisked us away.

The voices came into focus. I opened my eyes. We had landed and most of the passengers had already gotten off. Lohra gave me a longing smile and stood to leave. I waited until she was gone. My legs were too weak to stand.

Thankfully, by the time I got to the mini-van the only open seat was in the front. Back at the tent, I breezed past the champagne reception and went directly to the car. I drove into Friedrichshafen, found a Movenpick restaurant, and ran to the bank of Deutsche Telekom phones. The digital clock in the hallway showed 13:25, which made it 7:25 AM back home. Lisa would be leaving for work in five minutes. I quickly pulled out my phone card and punched in the numbers.

Busy signal. Anna! I tried again and again, always busy. What did teenage girls have to say that was so important it couldn't wait twenty more minutes until they saw each other at school? Another mystery of the universe only the next life will reveal.

I smiled at the image of my little angel curled up on the sofa, phone melded to her ear, talking a blue streak with a friend. I couldn't wait to get back home.

I entered the restaurant and ordered the special: *Spargel mit kase und schinken*. It was asparagus season, and there is nothing like fresh asparagus and smoked Black Forest ham smothered in melted cheese—and a fresh-brewed German lager to wash it down.

That appetite sated, I drove to the ferry, crossed the lake to Kreuzlingen, and headed for Schaffhausen. I had always wanted to see the Rhine Falls. It was early May and the snowmelt from the Alps rushed northward, through Lake Konstanz, and over a small but stupendous waterfall in the Rhine River. In the midst of the torrent stood a boot-shaped island. Small boats carried passengers to the tip of the island, where they could climb to the top of the boot for one of those you-have-to-see-it-to-believe-it experiences. I won't try to put words to the indescribable, just promise yourself to go see it someday.

On my way back through the concession area a book with an English title caught my eye: *Tales of Father Rhine*. Perfect for Cynthia! While standing in line to pay, I noticed the headline of a German newspaper. I couldn't resist translating it. "Rhine River Shipwreck First in Decades." The picture showed a barge grounded on some rocks near a place called St. Goar. The caption said, "Three men dead, ten missing." Hardened by years of American news media, all I felt was pride in my translation skills.

I paid for the book—along with a *Lion* candy bar, yum—and slowly strolled back toward the parking lot. From a nearby church floated the vibrant sounds of a women's choir singing Mozart's "Ave Verum." Heaven on earth.

I got back to Stuttgart late that night.

Lohra had stalked my thoughts all day.

And all night.

I barely made it to the airport in time. It took a full hour to pass through security, and the woman at the gate scowled at me as if she could sense my thoughts of infidelity. I was the last to board the plane.

I looked at every passenger as I worked my way through the aisles. Who was I looking for? Part of me wanted to see Lohra's alluring face, but the most important part of me dreaded the thought. An elderly woman had already settled into the seat next to mine. I closed my eyes and sighed with relief, then gasped as Lohra's image flooded my mind—Lohra, frolicking nude in the waves... *Help!* Desperate, I imagined my elderly seat partner in her birthday suit. I grimaced, shuddered, and then smiled in victory as I stowed my carry-on beneath the seat in front of me. Exhausted from the assault on my self-control, I collapsed into my seat.

Which brings us to where I started. And I fear it is truly just the start.

My elbow bumped the elderly German woman seated next to me. "Entschuldigen Sie bitte gnädige Frau."

"Certainly. How nice to hear an American speak German, and

with such good manners."

"Thank you, and your English is excellent. Would you care to see a picture of my family?"

"What a nice looking family you have. And such a beautiful wife. You must be very happy."

Exhausted from my trip, I slipped into that half-awake state that passes for sleep on an airplane.

Visions of Sugarplum Lohras danced in my head...

Maybe if I read a book or something. I retrieved *Tales of Father Rhine* from my bag and flipped on the overhead reading light.

I devoured the tales of Siegfried and Fafnir the dragon. Alberich and the Rhine maidens. The ring of the Niebelung. So many inspirations for Wagner's magnificent cycle of operas. And the story of Lorelei, a beautiful young maiden who, in a fit of despair over her faithless lover, threw herself into the river and drowned. She was transformed into a siren, and over the centuries her beautiful song lured countless helpless sailors to their deaths on the rocks.

I sniffed, shook my head, and closed the book. It was a shame they weren't carrying pictures of their families with them. I opened my wallet and savored the photos. I couldn't wait to get home!

Gingerly, I allowed a fleeting thought of Lohra to pass through my mind. Good. A twinge of desire, but nothing like that previous craving. I was ready for a stronger test. Might as well go for the big one. I recalled the image of her entrance on the zeppelin. My heart didn't miss a beat. Okay, it did pick up its pace a bit. I'm only human.

Confident the obsession had passed, I pulled the folded slip of paper with Lohra's address from where I had stashed it in my wallet. I chuckled. Did I really think I would ever dare to visit her? I crumpled the paper and stuffed it into the seat pocket in front of me, right behind the barf bag.

The elderly woman next to me snored softly. I had already seen the in-flight movie. After watching an episode of *C.S.I.* (in German, what a hoot), I decided to get my camera out and review the photos I had taken on my outing. The Minolta's two-inch screen was big enough to allow me to sort through and delete the losers. There were some poorly framed and out of focus shots, but more than enough dazzlers to amaze my friends and family when I got back.

Then I got to the photo the stewardess had taken.

It was a lovely picture of me, wide-eyed, with Lindau in the background. She had even managed to get the lighthouse and the Thieves' Tower in the corner of the shot.

It was a lovely picture of me, wide-eyed, with Lindau in the background.

A picture of me. Lindau.

Where was Lohra?

I punched the button advancing to the next picture: the Rhine Falls from the landing next to the castle. I went back two shots: a picture of the Bregenz Theater at a distance. I rubbed my eyes and advanced to the photo of me with Lohra.

It was a lovely picture of me, wide-eyed, with Lindau in the background.

How could that be? I zoomed the frame to the spot Lohra had occupied. All the pixels were there. And they were of Lindau.

Had I imagined her?

I stared at the camera. No Lohra.

The paper!

I clawed for the seat pocket and scrabbled through it. There it was. I carefully pulled the balled-up paper from the pocket. My hands trembled. I unwrinkled the paper and smoothed it flat on my lap. I took a very deep breath and read. It was as if I could hear Lohra's dulcet tones as my eyes passed over her words:

My dearest Jason,

I do hope you will bring your family for a visit. I want so much for you to hear me sing. You can find my island by taking a boat or plane and heading toward the middle of the triangle between Bermuda, Florida, and Puerto Rico. You'll know you are there when you hear me singing. I'll be waiting for you.

Love, Lorelei

During one orchestra rehearsal, I watched one of the violinists as she sawed her way through a difficult passage, her face the epitome of concentration. The music stopped, she lowered her instrument, and her face brightened as she smiled and exchanged comments with her stand partner. That was the inspiration for this story.

Her Face

I was minding my own business. Really. But I am a man, after all. What does she expect? She has taken the time to French braid her hair, and she has used only a tasteful hint of makeup. I'd bet she even spent some time in front of her closet selecting just the right blouse to go with that slinky skirt. Surely she must know men will look.

She turns. She is heading in my direction. I do a quick about face and stroll for cover behind a shelf of encyclopedias. I remove the "E" volume of World Book, then nudge a fat dictionary out of the way on the opposite side of the shelf. I have a straight view through the books. Perfect.

She takes a seat at a long table and pulls some things out of her tote bag. Let's see... Dobson's *Dare to Discipline*...and...*Child Psychology for Educators*. Hmm. Brains and beauty. Could be dangerous.

So what *is* it about her that turns me into a skulking voyeur?

Her face.

I know she can't see me, so I savor a lingering look. Oops. She glances around the room. I should know by now. Every woman has that sixth sense that tells her when a man is looking.

Good. She is back to her studies.

Oh... Now I see the minor flaws, the imperfections. When she ponders, the corners of her mouth droop, her eyes lose their luster. The color fades from her cheeks. Her long brown hair has no sheen. Even the lines of the braids look severe. Her nose is straight and protrudes just a bit too far.

Then she looks up aimlessly—and smiles.

Everything changes.

I witness a resurrection, like the high speed, time lapse video of a brilliant tulip as it bursts through the ground and leaps into bloom.

What is it about that smiling face?

Her eyes? They are hazel. Hazel? I don't remember seeing that color in my box of *Crayolas*. Maybe it's Greek or Latin for "never the same," or "wouldn't you like to know?" Now her eyes gleam as if the Creator again said, "Let there be light!" Tiny lines accent the corners of her eyes and point the way to perfect cheekbones, flushed with a tinge of pink. Her lips glisten as they part in a resplendent smile.

Her hair catches the sun spilling through the window. Wisps of blonde play hide and seek among the light brown tresses. She scoops a wandering lock of hair behind her ear, and a delicate pinky brushes against her ear lobe. Ah, that supple lobe, begging for a meaningful caress. That graceful neck, yearning for a kiss.

She shakes her head, gives a bemused grin, and leans back over her book. The drape of her blouse reveals that sacred hollow between her breasts. It calls to me. I am no longer my own.

I forsake my hiding place, go around the shelf, and cross toward her table. It is too late to turn back. Though she does not look up, I know her sixth sense announces my coming. But there is no longer any place for secrecy. I don't care if the whole world knows.

I boldly walk up behind her, lean down, and offer the gentlest of whispers in her ear. "Come away with me."

She doesn't look up. Her hair masks her face. I brace myself for her response.

She turns and meets my gaze. My heart does a somersault. She is glowing. "What about the kids?"

"I got a sitter."

"Can we afford all that?"

"I got a raise."

"Let's go." She flips her book closed, scoops her things into the tote bag, and leaps to her feet. She links her arm in mine and we are off.

The dinner isn't anything special.

But her face in the candlelight...

Bio

Sorry, I thought I was finished, but the publisher called and said I must write one more page. I had no idea readers expect a biography page like this, but if you do, then I must comply.

Let's see, what can I say that isn't common knowledge? Who doesn't already know about Lancelot and Guinevere, Camelot and the Round Table, Merlin and—

Hold on a second, gotta answer the phone.

Ohhh...

An *author's* bio. As if you didn't already learn more about me than you cared to know during the first 125 pages of this book.

I enjoy long walks on the beach—but not if I'm wearing sandals, flip-flops, shoes, or anything else on my feet. Walking in the rain is OK, as long as it isn't too windy and the temperature is just right. Oh, and if I'm walking in the rain with someone else, I'd rather use one big umbrella than two little ones because one of us is likely to get poked in the eye and I think that would most likely be me, and if it was the other person who got poked, I'd feel terribly guilty.

I have five delightful grandsons, all age five or under, and a sixth grandchild due later this year. Last March I babysat for three of my grandsons at the same time. All went well during the day, but the night was filled with pitiful sobs, bed-wetting, nightmares, and cries of "I want my Mommy!" Fortunately, all three grandsons slept soundly through the night.

Hold on, there's that danged phone again...

All right, all right. So I guess I have to write the type of info you'd find on a resumé.

Although I attended the Hanover public schools up through my sophomore year, I graduated from nearby Southwestern H.S. in 1971. I earned a B.S. in Music Education from The King's College in 1976 and a Master of Music in Low Brass Performance[44] from Ithaca College in 1978. I did additional coursework in conducting and brass pedagogy at Vandercook College of Music in Chicago, 1982-84; and I was awarded a doctoral fellowship to study conducting at Northwestern University in 1985.

My education experiences on the other side of the desk included ten years at Schoharie H.S. (band director, ensembles, music theory, general music, lessons); five years at The College of St. Rose (Wind Ensemble, conducting class, orchestration class, brass techniques, and supervisor of student teachers); and five years at Hartwick College (Adjunct Low Brass Professor.) I also served two

---

[44] "Low brass" refers to the bass trombone, euphonium, and tuba; this is not a musician stereotype.

terms on the Executive Council of the New York State School Music Association (NYSSMA).

On Broadway, I've appeared in the audience for more than forty hit musicals. Internationally, I've appeared at a wide variety of performances in Mexico, Canada, England, Italy, Germany, Austria, and Switzerland.

Conducting experiences include founding and conducting the Schoharie Valley Concert Band (1979-87), directing the choir at Pineview Community Church, Albany, N.Y. (1989-93), and several guest conducting appearances with All-County bands in upstate New York.

Maybe I'll write a book someday about my experiences as a soloist and conductor.[45] I'd have to give it a title that is the opposite of *Life in the Pits*, though. Maybe I should call it *Life on the Throne*— that is also the perfect title for a bathroom reader.[46] Shameless plugs for my other books appear on pages 125-128.

I've saved my grandest achievement for last. I was *TIME* magazine's Person of the Year for 2006. (I am not making this up.)

"One of these things is not like the others."

Jonathan, Nathan, Frank, Betsy, and Christopher Meredith, 1997.

---

[45] I've performed solos as a vocalist and on euphonium, bass trombone, tuba, trumpet, tenor recorder, and whip. Yes, whip. Guess I better write that book.

[46] I'm just fulfilling the Low Brass Players Union requirement to include a second bit of toilet humor in any book exceeding 100 pages in length.

Further Listening and Viewing

I know it will be tedious to type these links into a browser, but I hope you take the time; I believe you will find it was well worth the effort.

"Carmen Fantasy" for euphonium and piano, Bastien Baumet
www.youtube.com/watch?v=oOJ4dwLd0l8

Jazz funk with contrabassoon
www.youtube.com/watch?v=FacquMTkmoU

Cimbasso D'Amore: Classic love songs from Italy, performed on the cimbasso with a chamber music ensemble at Kean University's Enlow Recital Hall on November 1st, 2009.
http://media.kean.edu/vid/media/cimbasso-damore

Robert de Visée "Prélude et Allemande," Jonas Nordberg, theorbo
www.youtube.com/watch?v=qeUcGD4rRRc

"Game of Thrones Theme" performed by 23 trombones, bass trombones, contrabass trombones, cimbassos, and tubas.
www.youtube.com/watch?v=vTDEVUlCClk&feature=youtu.be

"Flight of the Bumblebee" on bass trombone. Jason Sulliman and the Terre Haute Symphony
This video is a "must see" for aspiring bass trombonists. It displays all the techniques you must acquire if you want to succeed in the business.
www.youtube.com/watch?v=YfCpLypa7qI

Read This Page Last!

Your Name is on this Page

To find your name, follow these simple instructions.

1) If your name is usually written with characters or in a different alphabet, you *must* transliterate it into English.

2) Cut out the letters in your name, then paste or tape them onto the lines provided.

3) Better yet, cut the letters out and paste them anywhere in the book where you would like to be part of the story. Feel free to purchase additional copies so you can enjoy being in many stories throughout the book!

First Name	Last Name

FIRST NAME

AAAA BBBB CCCC DDDD EEEE FFFF GGGG HHHH

IIII JJJ KKK LLLL MMMM NNNN OOOO PPPP

QQ[47] RRRR SSSS TTTT UUU VVV WWW XXX

YYY ZZZ

LAST NAME

AAAA BBBB CCCC DDDD EEEE FFFF GGGG HHHH

IIII JJJ KKK LLLL MMMM NNNN OOOO PPPP

QQ RRRR SSSS TTTT UUU VVV WWW XXX

YYY ZZZ

---

[47] If you have more than two Q's in one of your names, you deserve a free book.

Available in the following editions:
Hard cover: 336 pages, more than 50 rare maps and illustrations
Soft Cover: 336 pages, more than 50 rare maps and illustrations
Large Print: 440 pages, text only, 16-point type, 8x10 soft cover
Kindle Edition: through Amazon.com
Order autographed copies from: *www.TheUnfinishedWork.com*

THE UNFINISHED WORK
by Frank Meredith

June, 1863. Confederate troops invade Pennsylvania intent on winning their 2nd War of Independence, and young Jake Becker must choose: fight for southern freedom and earn the love of his Virginia belle, or defend his home and fight to end slavery? His decision puts him front and center at several pivotal events in the Gettysburg Campaign, where he discovers his ultimate call is to an even higher duty.

Like "The Killer Angels," "The Unfinished Work" features vivid, eyewitness accounts of participants on both sides of the battle lines. As in "Gone with the Wind," Eliza, a pampered southern belle, must cope with the life-changing consequences of the war, watch her lover go off to join the fight, and deal with the most unexpected rival for his affections – her sister, Kathleen.

Reviewers say . . .

"Meredith, drawing on extensive historical research, paints a vivid recreation of the Gettysburg campaign as seen by men on both sides of the battle line. The author's fictional creations are colorfully three-dimensional. Eliza, in particular, is a glorious confection of self-pity, insecurity and sugarcoated chutzpah, a downscale Scarlett O'Hara. An entertaining, human-scale rendering of the Gettysburg cataclysm." -- *Kirkus Discoveries*

"This novel is clearly written with a keen understanding of the culture of the 19th century Pennsylvania German farmers and residents, and the Civil War buff will appreciate the attention to historical detail, including some useful footnotes (unusual for a novelist to add this much appreciated touch.) For those readers who enjoy historical fiction, "The Unfinished Work" has broad appeal for both men and women, and it has an excellent storyline that holds the reader's attention." -- *Scott L. Mingus,* Sr., Civil War historian and author

"The battles were so finely crafted that you could almost smell the smoke and feel the heat of the blasts. The budding romance between Jake and the Bigler sisters brought welcome relief to the intensity of the battles and the emotions on both sides of the war. He easily made a case for the North and the South, leaving the choice of who was right up to the individual reader." -- *News and Experts*

Nomination for Franklin Award, Best Historical Fiction, 2010

The Battle of Gettysburg
As Seen by Two Teens:

The Stories of Tillie
Pierce and Daniel Skelly

edited by Frank Meredith

A great number of books have been written about the Battle of Gettysburg, but few of them contain the drama and emotion experienced firsthand by Tillie Pierce (a 15-year-old school girl), and Daniel Skelly (an 18-year-old store clerk.) Their eyewitness accounts are among the best civilian observations of the Civil War.

Twenty-five years later, Matilda "Tillie" Pierce Alleman self-published "At Gettysburg: What a Girl Saw and Heard of the Battle." Near the end of his life, Daniel Skelly wrote "A Boy's Experiences During the Battles of Gettysburg," which included the day Abraham Lincoln delivered his immortal "Gettysburg Address."

The full text of both stories appear together for the first time in this book, to which the editor has added dozens of historic photographs and maps to enhance the reader's experience.

Soft cover: 111 pages, 42 illustrations and maps
Kindle Edition: through Amazon.com
Available only through Amazon.com or from me at:
SavannahBooksInc@gmail.com
Discounts are available for bulk purchases.

63907310R00081

Made in the USA
Lexington, KY
22 May 2017